CONSTITUTIONAL LAW
AND LIABILITY FOR
PARK LAW ENFORCEMENT OFFICERS
THIRD EDITION

By

Dan S. Murrell, J.D., LL.M.
Cecil C. Humphreys School of Law
Memphis State University
Memphis, Tennessee 38152

and

William O. Dwyer, Ph.D.
Park Ranger Law Enforcement Training Program
Memphis State University
Memphis, Tennessee 38152

Carolina Academic Press
Durham, North Carolina

ACKNOWLEDGEMENTS

This book is dedicated to our wives, Pat and Judy, who continue to provide us with encouragement and inspiration.

The authors are also very grateful for the help of all those rangers, fish and wildlife officers, attorneys, graduate students and others who assisted us with advice, suggestions, and counsel during the development of this work. We wish to especially thank Ben Wages, Janna King, and Lisa Coleman for their assistance in research and editing, and Susan Vazquez for her final editing of the manuscript.

TO ORDER COPIES CONTACT:
Carolina Academic Press
700 Kent St.
Durham, North Carolina 27701
(919) 489-7486   FAX (919) 493-5668

TO THE READER------

This book is intended to help you, the reader, but we also need your help to insure that it meets your needs. If you have any suggestions, questions, problems, or situations that need to be addressed, please let us know so that we may consider those problems for future editions. We will try to respond individually to your correspondence.

We would like to know about your particular jurisdiction's laws, statutes, and regulations and will address those whenever possible in the future.

Any correspondence should be sent to either of the authors:

Professor Dan S. Murrell
Cecil C. Humphreys School of Law
Memphis State University
Memphis, Tennessee 38152
(901) 678-3219

or

Professor William O. Dwyer
Park Ranger Law Enforcement Training Program
Memphis State University
Memphis, Tennessee 38152
(901) 678-2149

NOTE: Blank pages have been left at appropriate intervals for your notes and questions.

TABLE OF CONTENTS

TABLE OF CASES

CHAPTER I

INTRODUCTION

The role of law enforcement in America's parks and recreation areas has shown a steady increase in recent years. At federal, state and local levels it is no longer uncommon to see rangers or park police officers patrolling park areas to protect the visitors as well as the resources they came to enjoy. Like officers in other settings, park law enforcement officers must abide by constitutional guidelines and mandates in their encounters with park visitors. As is the case for other officers, if park law enforcement officers violate these guidelines in their dealings with the public, they face the potential consequences of suppressed evidence as well as personal criminal and civil liability.

The purpose of this book is to provide a quick and handy reference for park law enforcement officers, fish and game wardens or officers, and other land management officers on how the Constitution, as interpreted through various court decisions, influences their contacts with visitors in the park or refuge setting. Of course, the general rules are essentially the same as they would be for any police officer; yet park law enforcement personnel operate in a unique environment that sometimes makes the application of case law somewhat difficult and confusing, but may also give them more latitude in policing. Our intention is to provide a sound framework against which the practice of park and land management law enforcement may be measured. The book is not meant to be a complete list of "Do's and Don'ts" because various state laws and local regulations, as well as agency guidelines and procedures, may also have a bearing on the breadth of enforcement authority given park rangers or park police officers or other land management law enforcement officers. Therefore, where more restrictive guidelines are in place, the reader is cautioned to make a note of them and abide by them.

CHAPTER II
LIABILITY AND CIVIL RIGHTS

A. BACKGROUND

Regardless of its form, a fundamental element of leisure is the perception of freedom. Visitors come to a park or recreation area to enjoy personal liberty; part of this enjoyment is the absence of interference by law enforcement figures. Rather, it entails the security to enjoy uninterrupted freedom (including the freedom to assemble peacefully and petition the government for redress of grievances). Thus, most park managers speak in terms of "low-key" law enforcement; doing the least possible to gain compliance with laws and regulations. On the other hand, park visitors also bring with them an "expectation of security and privacy"; they expect to be safe in their persons and their property. If loss or injury to visitors is reasonably foreseeable by park management, a host of recent court cases suggests that management must act to remedy the problem. And yet, if in its zeal to protect the public and the park's resources, park law enforcement unnecessarily impinges on visitors' civil rights or their expectations of privacy, the public is certain to seek remedy for what it perceives as a violation of its prerogatives.

Unlike most other police officers, park rangers, park police, and other land management officers serve as stewards over the areas in which they enforce the law, a condition that places on them a unique set of expectations from the public. Also unlike other law enforcement officers, park rangers and park police are typically exposed to increased administrative and political remedies which may be used by visitors who feel that they were mistreated. All these factors add up to a requirement for the professional and temperate use of police powers by park and recreation area officers. Of the various means that have been created for guaranteeing the protection of the public's constitutional rights, criminal and civil liability are of greatest concern to officers and administrators.

2

Although the Supreme Court has held that law enforcement officers enjoy a certain "qualified good-faith immunity" from liability for their actions, they may still be held criminally and civilly liable if they act outside the scope of their employment, contrary to their agency's guidelines, or if they violate a person's civil rights.

B. CRIMINAL LIABILITY

Several state and federal statutes make it a criminal offense for anyone acting in the capacity of a public law enforcement officer to willfully violate an individual's civil rights that are guaranteed by the United States Constitution or federal law. For example, Title 18 of the United States Code, Section 242, makes it illegal for an officer acting under color of law to willfully subject any inhabitant of a state, territory or district to the "deprivation of any rights, privileges or immunities secured or protected by the Constitution or laws of the United States. . . ." Thus, park law enforcement officers who willfully and with specific intent violate someone's civil rights may be convicted of a crime and imprisoned. Of course, for this to occur, they would have to be proven guilty beyond a reasonable doubt.

C. CIVIL LIABILITY

Various state governments as well as the federal government have established provisions for people who have been deprived of their civil rights by officers acting under color of law to sue those officers in civil court for compensation for any losses (including losses of a right) or harm which may have resulted from the deprivation. Title 42, Section 1983 of the U.S. Code, for example, states that anyone acting under color of law who "subjects, or causes to be subjected, any citizen of the United States or other person within the jurisdiction thereof to the deprivation of any rights, privileges or immunities secured by the Constitution and laws, shall be liable to the party injured in an action at law, lawsuit in equity, or other proper proceeding for redress." To be successful in such a suit, a plaintiff would not have to prove willfulness on the part of the officer, and the level of proof required is merely "a preponderance of the evidence" and not "beyond a reasonable doubt."

Increase in §1983 Lawsuits

Number of §1983 cases in the federal courts from 1955 through 1990

NOTES

CHAPTER III

REVIEW OF POLICE POWERS

A. THE CONSTITUTION AND POLICE AUTHORITY

In the last thirty years, the Supreme Court has energetically articulated (and restricted) the latitude within which law enforcement officers may exercise their police authority. The Court's decisions have had a significant impact on most aspects of police activity. Of course, most of these decisions have had their foundations in the first eight of the Ten Amendments, known as the Bill of Rights. Of the 23 rights guaranteed in these eight Amendments, 12 have a direct bearing on criminal procedure, and of these, the Fourth, Fifth, and Sixth Amendments are the most relevant for park law enforcement.

The **Fourth Amendment** (1) protects people against unreasonable searches and seizures, and (2) restricts the conditions under which warrants may be issued. The **Fifth Amendment** (1) requires a grand jury in criminal cases, (2) protects against double jeopardy, and (3) prohibits a person from being forced to testify against himself. The **Sixth Amendment** addresses the rights of individuals in criminal prosecutions: (1) the right to a speedy and public trial, (2) the right to an impartial jury, (3) the right to be informed of the charges against the defendant, (4) the right to subpoena witnesses, (5) the right to confront the accuser, and (6) the right to counsel.

Although the **First Amendment** does not bear directly on criminal procedure as such, it does guarantee five specific rights, two of which are quite relevant to law enforcement activities in park areas: (1) freedom of speech and (2) freedom of peaceable assembly. There may also be some instances in which an individual or individuals wish to exercise their freedom of religion.

What follows in this book is an elaboration on how the courts' interpretations of some of these rights have established the limits on what you, as a park ranger, law enforcement officer, or similar land or game management officer, are able to do as an agent of authority.

B. OFFICER AUTHORITY

What are police powers?

Police powers are inherent in the state governmental function and are granted to the federal government by the United States Constitution; they provide the authority and responsibility for designated governmental agents to provide for peace and order, to enforce the law, to detain and arrest others, and to seize property as evidence pursuant to knowledge of the commission of some crime.

What is the difference between the arrest power of citizens and that of public law enforcement officers?

Citizens possess the right to arrest perpetrators of crimes, but if after such an arrest, it is determined that the arrestee did not commit the crime, or the state does not prosecute, the arresting citizen may be liable for false arrest. On the other hand, a law enforcement officer employed by a public entity has certain immunity from such liability because, unlike the citizen who must have absolute knowledge (unless given special statutory authority) that the person to be arrested actually committed the crime, all that is required of a law enforcement officer (i.e., a person who is operating under color of law) is that he or she had probable cause to believe that a crime was committed and the person arrested committed it. Minor variations may exist among the different jurisdictions.

What is "good-faith immunity"?

Historically officers of the sovereign were given immunity under the theory that the sovereign could do no wrong. Today courts continue to recognize that, in order to do their jobs effectively, law enforcement officers require a certain amount of immunity from the consequences of their actions. This immunity, however, is qualified; it requires that the officer be acting in good faith. Like many concepts in law, "good faith" does not have an official definition, but in general terms it refers to an officer's behaving in a reasonable manner that is based on a reasonable level of training and possession of skills. In other words, it is not enough merely for you to think that you are doing right. Your actions must meet the standard of what a reasonable and adequately trained officer would be likely to do in the situation. Of course, in the last analysis, a jury will make that final judgment if the matter is contested in court.

What is "probable cause"?

Probable cause refers to a level of certainty. It means you must have more reason to believe than not that a particular person committed a particular crime, or that evidence of a crime is in a particular place.

Who is operating under "color of law"?

For the purpose of exercising police authority, any person who is (or has the appearance of being) employed by a public entity for the purpose of enforcing laws, or supervising those enforcing laws, regulations or ordinances, preventing and detecting crime, and apprehending criminals is working under color of law. This also includes persons protecting parks, plants, trees, and wildlife, if given such enforcement responsibility.

Some park jurisdictions employ uniformed personnel who appear to be rangers but are not "commissioned". These individuals may be assigned to campgrounds or even to "non-enforcement" patrol activities. The National Park Service, as an example, employs uniformed people who are given a "Park Protection Designation"; they are authorized to write citations only for certain minor violations. For purposes of constitutional guarantees regarding arrest, search and seizure, and other civil rights, such people are probably acting under color of law. Similarly, park systems that employ uniformed patrol rangers on an unarmed, non-commissioned basis until they have completed law enforcement training are normally placing them under the mantle of color of law, a status that has definite implications in terms of criminal and civil liability (e.g., 18 USC §242 and 42 USC §1983 could come into play). It may also give them some protection under the sovereign immunity umbrella.

The general rule is that if, through your appearance, talk or actions, you appear to visitors to have police authority, then you are probably acting under color of law. This is true, whether or not you have been given statutory or administrative authority to enforce the law.

What is the significance of being a "sworn" law enforcement officer?

In terms of your status with regard to color of law or your law enforcement authority, whether or not you were "sworn in" as a law enforcement officer has little bearing on your discretion or your authority. The issue is whether or not you were hired to enforce the law and prevent, detect, and investigate crime.

Who has the authority to exercise police powers under color of law?

Authority refers to what you can properly do as a law enforcement officer. It is granted either through specific state or federal statutes or, in some cases, through common law. It is essential that you be familiar with the source and the scope of your authority as a park law enforcement officer.

What if I hold law enforcement commissions from more than one jurisdiction?

As an example, you are a U.S. Fish and Wildlife Refuge officer, and you have also been commissioned by the local sheriff to assist in enforcing state game laws in the area. Multiple commissions means that you have been given police authority to enforce the relevant laws and regulations of the various jurisdictions that commissioned you. It is, however, not a guarantee that, should you become exposed to criminal or civil liability as a result of your police actions, those other jurisdictions will provide for your defense or pay any judgments against you. Because of these potential problems, multiple commissions are generally a good thing to avoid.

C. PARK JURISDICTION

What is jurisdiction?

Jurisdiction normally refers to a territorial boundary within which a sovereign's authority may be legally exercised. It is usually articulated (restricted or expanded) in statutory language. Jurisdiction in criminal matters either exists or it does not, and it may never be waived. Regarding any law of a particular jurisdiction, a person either violated it or did not. Officers, therefore, either have the legal authority to act or they do not, and could easily become criminally and civilly liable for kidnapping, false imprisonment, robbery, etc., if they exercised police powers without appropriate jurisdictional authority. Whereas authority refers to <u>what</u> you may do, jurisdiction refers to the location or origin of the crime. You should be familiar with your jurisdiction and avoid acting outside of it.

Is there more than one type of jurisdiction?

Some park agencies, like the National Park Service, must deal with more than one type of special jurisdiction, which means that within a given park, rangers may have different types of authority in different locations of the park. This special jurisdiction may be EXCLUSIVE, meaning that one entity (e.g., the federal government) has sole authority over it. It may be CONCURRENT, meaning that two or more entities (e.g., the federal government and a particular state government) are each able to enforce their own laws in it, even with respect to the same act (e.g., poaching a deer or a duck). It may be PARTIAL, which is similar to EXCLUSIVE except that a second entity retains jurisdiction with respect to certain laws or rights (e.g., hunting laws). Finally, jurisdiction may be PROPRIETARY, which is actually not a true jurisdiction. It means that, although a particular entity may own the property, it has no jurisdiction to enforce laws with respect to the territory. It may be able, however, to enforce certain regulations or laws with respect to property (e.g., destruction of government property). You should be very familiar with the type of jurisdiction your agency has over the park property you have been assigned to patrol.

If I work in an area of concurrent jurisdiction, may I enforce the laws of the other jurisdiction, even though I am not commissioned by the other jurisdiction and do not work for it?

Not directly; your arrest, search and seizure powers flow from the authority granted by your own jurisdiction. But, if the other jurisdiction has a relevant law covering the offense, you may request that the other jurisdiction initiate a prosecution. As an example, you are a National Park ranger working in a park with concurrent jurisdiction, and you arrest a suspect for breaking into a motor vehicle and stealing camera equipment. You notify the United States Attorney, who decides not to prosecute the case. You may then ask the state district attorney to initiate a state prosecution, even though you are a federal officer. Similarly, if you are a state park ranger and make a narcotics arrest involving a significant quantity of drugs, you may want to approach the United States Attorney to initiate a prosecution in federal court. You should work out the details regarding the correct procedure for getting such prosecutions initiated before you actually have occasion to make use of it.

What if I intervene in some criminal activity outside of my agency's jurisdiction and outside the normal scope of my authority?

As an example, what if a U.S. Fish and Wildlife Refuge Officer intervenes in the robbery of a local service station? It is important that you understand your particular state's law on this issue. Some states convey the status of "peace officer" on all law enforcement personnel, and expect you to intervene, especially in a felony. Other states do not have such a law and you would be "on your own" should you become involved (unless, of course, it was at the specific request of an officer with the proper authority). Regardless of the particular authority conferred on you in such situations, you should have the answer to two very important questions: (1) If my actions lead to some criminal or civil liability, who is going to pay for my defense? (2) If there is a financial judgment against me, who is going to pay the judgment?

If I am in uniform, do I still have my citizen's arrest powers?

Here again, you must become familiar with the laws of your particular state. In some states uniformed law enforcement officers give up their citizen's arrest powers. In most jurisdictions you have your police powers whether in or out of uniform.

D. LAWS AND REGULATIONS

Park rangers may be given the responsibility of enforcing both laws and regulations, sometimes of more than one jurisdiction.

What are criminal laws?

Criminal Laws designate certain acts or failures to act as being illegal and provide specific punishments for them. To be enacted, laws must be passed by either state or federal legislatures (depending upon jurisdiction) or have uncontested common law existence at the state level.

What are regulations?

Regulations may also articulate limits on behavior and may carry penalties of fines and imprisonment. Unlike laws, however, regulations are not specifically enacted by a legislature; rather they are promulgated by an agency (e.g., the Department of the Interior). Of course, the agency depends on legislation for its right to promulgate such regulations. Regulations can have the force and effectiveness of law; that is, their violation can lead to legal action, arrest, fines, and imprisonment.

E. DEADLY FORCE

RULE OF LAW: Deadly force may not be used to effect an arrest. It may be used only to protect yourself or others from imminent lethal force or severe injury.

For all federal rangers as well as rangers in many state systems, the question of when deadly force may be employed is fairly simple to answer; it may be applied only after all other reasonable means have been exhausted and in defense of the ranger's life or someone else's. Until 1985 some states allowed officers to shoot to stop fleeing felons. Since 1985, however, the Supreme Court has ruled that shooting a fleeing felon merely to prevent escape is a violation of civil rights.

Under what conditions may I use deadly force?

Specifically, the Supreme Court restricted the use of deadly force to situations of (1) defense of the officer's life, (2) defense of others' lives, or (3) when the officer has probable cause to believe that the suspect has committed a violent crime involving the infliction or threat of death or serious harm, or probable cause to believe that the suspect is armed and poses an imminent substantial risk to others. To be protected by qualified good faith immunity, you must follow the established deadly force policy of your agency, and if you are using deadly force (in accordance with policy) to stop a person under condition (3) above, you must exhaust all other reasonable means of apprehension and, whenever possible, identify yourself and warn suspects that if they do not stop you will use deadly force.

NOTES

CHAPTER IV

CONFRONTING THE SUSPICIOUS VISITOR

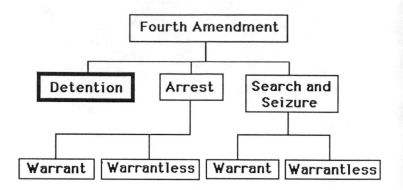

RULE OF LAW: You may stop a park visitor, even though you do not have an adequate cause for arrest, if you observe unusual behavior or circumstances which lead you to suspect that criminal activity may be occurring, has occurred or is about to occur, or if you believe that the visitor may be involved in injury to the park or in violation of park regulations. The stop is to allow you to confirm or eliminate your suspicions concerning the illegal activity.

A. STOPPING A VISITOR

When conducting a stop you must identify yourself or be identifiable as a park law enforcement officer. As a ranger or park police officer, you have a broader latitude to make a stop than do most other conventional officers, because of park interests and needs (e.g., the necessity for more rules and regulations). Of course, you must act with the discretion of a reasonable, good-faith park officer concerned with visitors' safety, their enjoyment of the park, and park security.

1. **Routine stops**: During a routine stop you may ask visitors about their conduct or that of others relative to your park concern, and you may detain visitors for a brief, but reasonable time, to facilitate the investigation or inquiry.

You may also hold items that were in possession of visitors (e.g., a hunting knife, a pack, etc.) for the duration of a reasonable stop.

You may stop suspicious visitors, whether they are on foot, bicycle, horseback, or in a vehicle, boat or other conveyance.

You may also observe all items in plain view during the stop and may seize any evidence, fruits, or instrumentalities of any crime. This observation may be aided by a flashlight beam. What you observe, hear, and smell during the stop may be used to help develop probable cause for an arrest or a search warrant.

When may I stop and question a visitor whose behavior or condition seems questionable?

In order to stop and question a visitor about possible illegal activity, you must have a **reasonable suspicion** that a crime has been, is being, or is about to be committed and that the person is somehow connected with it. Reasonable suspicion involves articulable facts or apparent facts that would lead a reasonable and prudent park ranger to believe that a crime may be taking place and that the suspicious person is involved. It must be more than a "hunch" or a "feeling" but does not necessarily have to meet the requirement of probable cause.

Mere suspicion, based on your sense or feeling for a situation, may cause you to make inquiries of a person, but gives you no authority to compel a stop, force someone to answer you, or even to conduct a "Terry" type frisk. In order to detain and frisk someone, you must have reasonable suspicion.

17

In an investigative stop, does a suspect have to answer my questions?

No. People are under no legal obligation to answer any of your questions. If they refuse to talk to you, you may NOT use this refusal as a reason to arrest. In other words, the exercise of a civil right cannot be used to help establish probable cause. For example, you are on patrol at night and you see someone walking along a park road alone. You ask him if he needs help and he says "No". You become suspicious and ask him his name and what he is doing. He tells you that it's none of your business. Without any other information, you cannot arrest him, nor can you force him to answer. If, however, you see that he has blood on his shirt or is carrying an unauthorized weapon, etc., you may continue the stop a reasonable amount of time for further investigation.

2. **Roadblocks**: Roadblocks may be used in certain situations to search vehicles going through a particular point. As an example, a roadblock could be used to search all vehicles exiting a campground for the purpose of looking for a missing child, or exiting the park during hunting season for the purpose of looking for illegal game, etc. A roadblock may be used for systematic and directed checks of permits, licenses, etc. You should not look where you are not likely to find the object of the search. If, for example, you are checking for hunting violations, it would normally be inappropriate to search in the vehicle's glove compartment. When the sought item is found, the roadblock should be dismantled.

During the stop, all items that you observe in plain view that you believe to be the evidence, fruits, or instrumentalities of a crime may be properly seized. To justify the warrantless seizure of an item in plain view, the officer must not only be lawfully located in a place from which the object can be plainly seen, but the officer must also have a lawful right or access to the object itself.

Roadblocks should be as brief and unobtrusive as possible and should last no longer than necessary to accomplish the purpose.

May I establish a roadblock to stop every vehicle to check for such things as: illegal hunting activity, underage use of alcohol, or invalid operator's permits?

Yes. You may establish a roadblock for specific purposes when you suspect that particular criminal activity is occurring, such as illegal hunting or underage use of alcohol. Your roadblock should be limited to stopping those people who could be violators within the framework of your purpose. As an example, you should not stop older persons when searching for youth. The key is to keep the intrusion to a minimum. Searching for invalid operator's permits should normally be by departmental or agency plan and be very directed.

While it is not necessary, you can always seek a warrant to establish a roadblock. This judicial scrutiny of your activity satisfies the bulk of the constitutional mandates and helps to protect your actions and any evidence that may be seized.

May I establish roadblocks to stop certain classes of vehicles (e.g., pickup trucks, vans, or vehicles being driven by juveniles) to check for such things as underage alcohol use or illegal hunting?

Yes. You may stop certain classes of vehicles so long as there is a clear purpose and not a general "fishing expedition" or arbitrary action. For example, you could stop all vehicles pulling boats if you have reason to believe that illegal fishing activity has occurred.

May I establish a roadblock to stop every vehicle that matches the description of one used in a recent crime in the vicinity?

Yes. You may establish a roadblock stopping all vehicles, in whatever form, that match the description of the vehicle involved in suspected or actual criminal activity. The intrusion and delay time should always be kept to a minimum but may be of sufficient time for adequate inquiry. Once it is determined that the vehicle or occupants are not involved, the vehicle should be released and the investigation should not proceed into other areas unless plain view evidence gives rise to appropriate further inquiry. Once the object of the search, vehicle, or person is seized, the roadblock must be dismantled for that purpose, although it could be converted for other specific purposes, such as discovery of a new crime or offenders, etc.

You may also establish a roadblock stopping all vehicles with occupants, either by number or appearance, similar to those suspected of committing a crime in the area.

May I establish a moving roadblock for which I patrol along roads and stop certain classes of vehicles (e.g., pickups) to check for such things as underage alcohol use or hunting violations?

Yes, if the purpose matches the vehicle or its occupants as described above.

May I set up a roadblock in which I systematically stop a certain proportion of the vehicles (e.g., every fifth one) to check for such things as illegal hunting activity, illegal use of alcohol, or invalid driver's licenses?

Yes, if your plan is systematic and the purpose matches the plan, or the vehicle or its occupants as described above. As a reminder, you cannot stop vehicles on an arbitrary basis.

While effecting a traffic stop, may I make the driver get out of the vehicle?

Yes. Without any further justification, you may routinely order the driver of a vehicle you have stopped to get out of the vehicle during your encounter. Unless public safety dictates, however, you may not order a person to re-enter the vehicle. For example, you may not order a visitor to return to the vehicle after exiting it during a traffic stop, unless it is necessary to move the vehicle. The same would generally hold true for passengers who exit the vehicle. Unless there is a clear safety need, you could not order them to get back into the vehicle.

May I check the VIN during a stop at a roadblock?

Yes, you may check the VIN (vehicle identification number) during any lawful stop whether at a roadblock or not. You may reach into the vehicle and move objects covering the VIN plate, and any evidence, fruits or instrumentalities of a crime discovered in the course of such action may be properly seized. The stop, under appropriate circumstances, such as looking for a particular stolen vehicle, may even be to check the VIN number.

May I establish a roadblock/checkpoint to stop every vehicle to check for an intoxicated driver?

Yes. Usually referred to as "OUI(DWI) checkpoints," they may be legally established to allow you to briefly stop every vehicle and talk to the driver to make sure he or she is sober enough to drive.

What are the conditions and restrictions of such a checkpoint?

To make sure that your checkpoint is being conducted in a manner consistent with guidelines enumerated by the Supreme Court, you should do the following:

a. Make a public announcement (e.g., in local newspapers) that you will be conducting such stops in the park over the next few weeks/months.
b. Establish a written policy in the park detailing the conduct of such checkpoints.
c. Obtain written directives from management for each checkpoint occurrence, detailing exactly where, when, and for what duration the checkpoint will be conducted.
d. Establish checkpoint locations that will maximize safety for the officers and motorists. Clearly identify them with signs, traffic cones, and adequate lighting.
e. Stops should be brief and courteous, requiring only a short conversation during which the ranger can look for signs of intoxication, such as presence of alcohol in vehicle, odor of an intoxicating beverage, quality of speech, general demeanor, etc.
f. If, based upon these observations, your suspicion is aroused that the driver may be intoxicated, the stop would then proceed as any other OUI (DWI) traffic stop.
g. Be sure to have adequate manpower present to handle more than one vehicle at a time, or any arrests, vehicle impoundments, etc. that may be required.
h. Do not let your checkpoint develop into a traffic jam. Drivers should not have to wait very long for you to contact them. If such a condition begins developing, it is wise to wave all of them through without contacting them.

3. Waterblocks

If my park has a problem with people boating while under the influence of alcohol, may I conduct "waterblocks" during which I check boat operators for sobriety?

Yes. You may conduct waterblocks for "boating under the influence," using the same basic criteria you would for roadblock OUI checkpoints. In addition to the other requirements, it would be wise to post a notice at area boat ramps informing boaters that you periodically conduct such stops. Remember that if you obtain reasonable suspicion that a boat operator may be intoxicated, the typical field sobriety tests requiring balance may be less useful on the water. Other types of tests should be considered.

B. FRISKING A SUSPECT

RULE OF LAW: During a stop, you may conduct a frisk to protect yourself or others if you have a reasonable suspicion that the individual stopped may be armed and dangerous.

1. Individual

A frisk of an individual is a patdown of the outer clothing for the sole purpose of looking for **weapons**. A frisk may also extend to the inside of an over garment, such as an overcoat. You may use the minimum reasonable force, excluding deadly force, necessary to compel submission to the frisk. As an example, this may include the use of handcuffs if they are necessary to restrain the suspect during a frisk.

What is "reasonable force"?

Reasonable force is that amount which is minimally necessary and which would be used by a reasonable and prudent officer to gain compliance from a suspect. Any amount of force above this level would be considered **punishment** and would, therefore, be excessive.

When may I frisk an individual whom I have stopped?

You may frisk suspects whom you have stopped only if you have a **reasonable** (that is, articulable) suspicion that they may be armed and that they may harm you or others. You do not need probable cause, but neither is a "hunch" or a "feeling" sufficient. Reasonable suspicion for a frisk is established essentially by a combination of the suspect's demeanor and the bulkiness of the clothing being worn.

May I conduct a "Terry" frisk on the beach?

Yes, if warranted. Remember, you are searching for weapons because you believe the person may be armed and dangerous. Thus, a person clothed only in a swimsuit would generally not meet this criterion.

If I stop a person on a ski slope, may I frisk him or her?

Yes, you may make a stop and frisk as if the person were on a trail or road. Your frisk could extend to the inside of the ski parka if necessary.

a. Articles taken during a frisk

What may I remove from a person whom I am frisking?

You may remove only those items that you reasonably suspect could be weapons. Examples would be: guns, knives, brass knuckles, nun-chuks, hair picks, screwdrivers and other tools, bottles, chains, etc. If, however, an object you believe to be a weapon is removed, but is not a weapon, yet it is evidence or fruits of a crime, it may be seized. Any item removed pursuant to a valid frisk, or observed in plain view during the frisk, that is evidence of a crime, may be used to support a subsequent arrest or warrant. Remember, you are responsible for any objects taken, and the individual should be told where he or she may recover them later, if they are not illegal to possess.

If, during a frisk, I feel something soft in a pocket, may I remove it?

No. A frisk is a patdown for weapons, only. As an example, while frisking a suspect, you feel something soft, remove it from his pocket, and it turns out to be cocaine. If you arrested him on a narcotics charge, the evidence seized may be suppressed at trial. Under some circumstances, however, the evidence may be used to support a Grand Jury indictment or search warrant. In any event, you may confiscate the cocaine because the individual may not lawfully possess it.

b. Frisking others

If I stop and frisk a person, may I frisk others who are with him?

You may frisk them if you believe that they are dangerous to you or others and that they may interfere with your initial stop and its purpose. The mere presence of others at the stop or frisk, however, does not necessarily justify a frisk of them.

c. Frisking the opposite sex

Is it permissible to frisk a suspect of the opposite sex?

From a constitutional perspective, there are no prohibitions about frisking persons of the opposite sex other than those rules which govern the frisking of any suspect. It is important, however, to keep in mind that you should never do anything that a court may consider sufficiently shocking or offensive to social norms, because it could result in your losing the case. Of course, you should abide by any additional guidelines which your agency may have on this issue. Do remember the purpose of frisking and act accordingly.

2. Area around suspect

You may extend the frisk to the immediate area around the stopped visitor if you feel that the visitor is dangerous and may be able to reach a weapon. This extension is solely for the purpose of looking for a weapon. You might, for example, pat down or reach and grab a weapon on the floor of an automobile, on the seat of a boat, on a blanket, or in a tent if it is in close proximity. The allowable extent of your search is essentially determined by the "jump and reach" rule (see page 42).

3. Examining possessions

If the suspect is in possession of a sleeping bag or backpack, may I look in these items for weapons during a frisk?

In general, the answer would be "No". For example, you stop hitchhikers who have sleeping bags strapped to their backpacks on their backs. You should not frisk the sleeping bags. However, if they are holding the sleeping bags, you could frisk the bags for weapons. As another example, while on back country patrol in an area known for its drug trafficking, you encounter a suspicious-acting individual carrying a backpack that appears to have a sharp, hard, object inside of it. You could frisk the pack for **weapons**, but you may not search for other items without additional cause. The frisk may, therefore, be extended to a patdown of a bedroll, pack, saddlebag, etc. In the park setting, the frisk may be used to remove legal weapons (e.g., a hunting knife), if you believe that such a course of action is reasonably necessary for your own protection during the stop. If you remove a legal weapon you must, of course, tell the person where it may be recovered.

NOTES

CHAPTER V

ARRESTING A PARK VISITOR

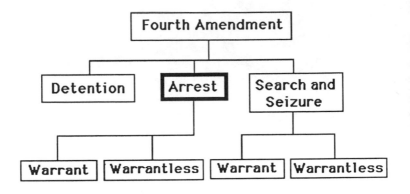

A. BACKGROUND

1. What is an arrest?

You have arrested a person when you have deprived him of his freedom to come and go by taking him into custody. Whether an arrest has been made is determined from the circumstances. The courts routinely say that an arrest has been made if several officers are standing around a person, the officer's gun is drawn, the person is taken to headquarters, etc. Obviously, a person is under arrest if told so; however, words are not necessary, as actions may indicate the occurrence of an arrest.

A person is not under arrest if he volunteers to come to park headquarters or to a police station to make a statement and then is free to leave.

Once I have arrested someone, may I release that person myself without the intervention of some judicial authority?

There is no process of unarrest. You may release an individual on your own initiative; however, you must be careful of the process because false arrest charges could be raised.

Of course, if you have merely stopped a person for investigation, releasing that individual is not a problem.

What is the difference between an arrest and a temporary investigative detention?

A temporary detention for investigation is exactly that - temporary - of short duration. The person is either quickly released or he is arrested. During a detention a "Terry" type frisk may be used to look for weapons if you have reason to believe that the suspect may be armed and dangerous.

An arrest involves depriving a person of freedom to come and go, that is, seizing the person. The arrest must be justified if you expect it to continue.

If I issue a citation, is that essentially the same thing as an arrest?

No, not unless you intend it to be and make the arrest pursuant to the probable cause giving rise to the citation or other probable cause. To make an arrest, physical custody must be involved. You may not search incident to a citation.

2. **Why arrest?**

What are the reasons for arresting a suspect?

In general, you would arrest a person whom you have probable cause to believe has committed a felony, or one who has committed a misdemeanor in your presence, and if you can satisfy any of the three following reasons: (1) to guarantee the person's presence in court, (2) to protect the person or someone else from physical harm, or (3) to prevent the loss or destruction of evidence of the crime. You should NOT arrest a violator "just to teach a lesson."

3. Requirements for an arrest

What are the requirements for a lawful arrest?

You must have the authority, you must be in the appropriate jurisdiction, and you must have a warrant or **probable cause** to believe that a crime was committed and the person you are about to arrest was the perpetrator.

Do I need a warrant to make an arrest?

In spite of the "warrant requirement" in the Fourth Amendment, you generally do not need a warrant to make a physical arrest for a felony or for a misdemeanor committed in your presence. However, it is a very good idea to obtain a warrant if you have time.

What is the difference between a felony and a misdemeanor?

A **felony** is any offense for which the penalty may exceed more than one year in jail. A **misdemeanor** is any offense for which the penalty is less than one year in jail. A **petit offense** is a type of misdemeanor for which the penalty is further limited.

4. Personal jurisdiction

Personal jurisdiction involves an officer's having physical control (custody) over a subject for the purpose of the judicial process.

Personal jurisdiction of an individual within your jurisdiction may be obtained

(a)   pursuant to an arrest
(b)   pursuant to a warrant
(c)   by consent or submission
(d)   by subpoena

Personal jurisdiction outside of your jurisdiction may be obtained

(a)   by consent or submission
(b)   through a federal warrant for unlawful flight to avoid prosecution (UFAP)
(c)   by extradition

If I want to obtain custody of a person who is outside of my jurisdictional boundary (e.g., over the state line), is it lawful for the other jurisdiction's officers to hand the subject over at the border?

While such expulsion is not the appropriate means to obtain personal jurisdiction of a suspect, the accused so acquired may still be lawfully tried. Evidence obtained pursuant to the arrest may be considered suppressible, however, and questions of liability for the arresting officers may arise.

Suppose that I am outside of my agency's jurisdiction and observe a suspect whom I know is wanted for a felony in my jurisdiction. May I properly arrest that person and return him or her to my jurisdiction?

You may take the suspected felon into custody for the local authorities; then appropriate authorities may take action for extradition. When you take the suspect into custody, you should turn him or her over to local authorities as soon as possible.

How long may I hold an arrestee before I must take him or her before a judge or magistrate?

As a general rule an in-custody suspect must be taken before a magistrate as soon as possible, and in no event later than within forty-eight hours. Some examples of delays even within the forty-eight hours which are unreasonable are delays for the purpose of gathering additional evidence to justify the arrest, a delay motivated by ill will against the arrested individual, or delay for the delay's sake. The government upon demonstration of a *bona fide* emergency may obtain a brief extension, but delays for administrative purposes, hearing consolidations, or intervening weekends do not qualify as extraordinary circumstances. The individual does not bear the burden of proving unreasonable delay, rather the government bears the responsibility of proving a *bona fide* emergency or extraordinary circumstance was present.

B. WARRANT ARRESTS

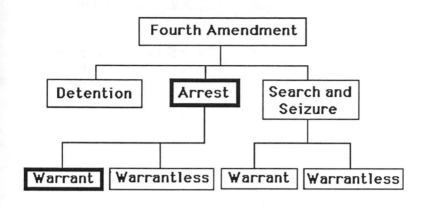

RULE OF LAW: A park ranger may arrest any person believed to be named in a valid arrest warrant. This arrest may be pursuant to the knowledge of a warrant even though the warrant is not in hand.

What is an arrest warrant?

An arrest warrant is an order from the issuing court directing an officer or class of officers (e.g., any Maine state game warden) to carry out a particular action, such as take an individual into custody.

What do I need to obtain a warrant for an arrest?

In order to obtain an arrest warrant from a judicial officer (e.g., a judge or magistrate), you will have to demonstrate that you have probable cause for the suspect's arrest for a particular crime. The facts or apparent facts you use to develop your probable cause will have to be presented to the judicial officer in sworn testimony, usually accompanied by a written complaint or affidavit.

If a judge issues an arrest warrant based on the information I provided, am I immune from any liability for an unconstitutional arrest?

Not necessarily. The Court has held that you are granted qualified good-faith immunity only if a reasonable officer would have believed that the facts you presented were adequate to establish probable cause. Thus, a judge's signature on a warrant does not necessarily protect you from liability.

From whom may I obtain an arrest warrant?

Generally arrest warrants may be obtained by appearing before any judge, magistrate, or justice of the peace, regardless of jurisdiction. However, it is advisable to seek an arrest warrant from the judge or magistrate associated with your particular jurisdiction. Federal warrants normally require the judge or magistrate to be of a court of record (i.e., as opposed to a justice of the peace).

When must I have a warrant to make a physical arrest?

Unless it is a true emergency, you must have a warrant to make an arrest under the following conditions:

1. when you are arresting persons in their own home or in the dwelling of another where they have a right to be.

2. when you are making an arrest for a misdemeanor not committed in your presence.

What are the restrictions regarding the execution of warrants from other jurisdictions, or in other jurisdictions?

If you are inside your park boundary you may:

1. execute an arrest warrant issued for your jurisdiction for an offense committed in your park area.

2.   execute an arrest warrant issued for your jurisdiction for an offense committed in another park area.

3.   hold a person for the proper authorities if you believe your jurisdiction or another jurisdiction issued an arrest warrant for a crime committed elsewhere.

If you are outside your park boundary but within your state you may:

1.   execute an arrest warrant issued by your jurisdiction for an offense committed in your park or in another park in your system.

2.   assist other officers in the execution of their warrants.

If you are outside your park boundary and outside your state you may:

1.   not execute any arrest warrants unless you are a federal officer (e.g., National Park ranger, U.S. Fish and Wildlife officer, National Forest ranger, etc.)

2.   assist other officers in the execution of their warrants.

If you are in a park with concurrent or proprietary jurisdiction you may:

1.   not execute warrants issued by the other jurisdiction, but if you are within the park boundary, you may

2.   hold the person named in the warrant for the proper jurisdiction. If such a detention is to be for more than a brief period of time, the suspect must be taken before an appropriate judicial officer of that jurisdiction.

C. Warrantless Arrests

RULE OF LAW: A park ranger may arrest, without a warrant, any person committing a misdemeanor in his or her presence or any person whom the ranger has probable cause to believe has committed a felony.

Do I have to observe visitors actually committing an offense before I may arrest them for it?

In general, the answer is "No" for felonies and "Yes" for misdemeanors.

If I don't actually observe the felony, what can I use to establish probable cause to arrest the offender?

Any facts or apparent facts which lead you to reasonably believe that the offender probably committed the offense can help develop probable cause. Examples would be: testimonies of others, lying during questioning, furtive activities, difficulty in making a vehicle stop, the presence of burglar tools, a physical description, or the smell of an intoxicating beverage about an individual. When any one fact (or group of facts) makes you believe that (1) a specific crime was probably committed and (2) a given person probably was involved in committing it, then you have probable cause for an arrest.

May a "feeling" or a "hunch" I have about a person help develop probable cause for an arrest?

No. You must have facts or apparent facts with which to develop probable cause.

May I use a person's refusal to answer my questions to help develop probable cause for an arrest?

No. The exercise of a civil right should not be used to help develop the basis for an arrest.

Can an arrest be justified by what I discover after the arrest has been made?

No. You must obtain all the information necessary to establish probable cause for an arrest before it is made. For example, if you arrest a park visitor without sufficient probable cause and subsequently discover that he has been selling cocaine in a campground, that discovery will not validate the arrest.

Under what conditions may I make an arrest for a misdemeanor?

1. if the arrest is pursuant to a warrant.

2. if the misdemeanor was committed in your presence.

3. in some jurisdictions, if you have a witness' signed statement or affidavit.

4. under certain conditions in which it is obvious that a suspect committed the misdemeanor, such as finding a drunk behind the steering wheel of a wrecked vehicle. While you did not witness the accident, conditions are sufficiently strong to support an arrest. State statutes

vary on this particular issue, and you should be familiar with the laws of your jurisdiction.

NOTES

CHAPTER VI

SEARCH INCIDENT TO ARREST

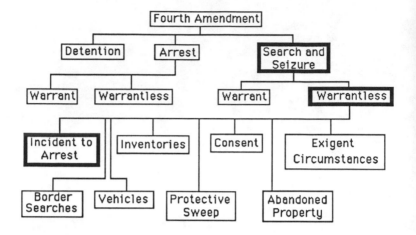

RULE OF LAW: A search may be made pursuant to a valid arrest if the search is contemporaneous in time and place with the arrest. The search includes the person of the individual arrested, the area immediately around the arrestee and items within his or her reach (the "jump and reach" rule).

While specifically allowed incident to arrest, the purpose of the search is to (1) protect the officer or others, (2) prevent the destruction of evidence, and (3) prevent escape or suicide. You should use the warrantless search incident to arrest carefully, because there is no "judicial eye" watching, and evidence you find may be suppressed, whereas it could have been admitted if it were obtained pursuant to a valid warrant. Also, you are prohibited from making a pretextual arrest just to allow a search incident to that arrest.

A. SEARCH OF THE INDIVIDUAL

If there is a valid arrest, you may properly perform a complete body search, excluding body cavities or a strip search, provided you do so immediately and at the place of the arrest. You may extend the time or move the location only for an urgent need, such as removing the person from a dangerous location where the search will not be interfered with by others. If you have justifiable grounds for doing so, you may remove a person to another area for a strip search. If you made the arrest, either you or persons assisting you may conduct the search. Others not involved, or involved at a later time, may not make the search which was to be performed at the arrest.

This prohibition does not inhibit custodial searches or searches by officers transporting suspects or prisoners. The purpose of such searches, however, is to protect the officer and prevent escape and is limited accordingly. Any evidence found pursuant to such a search may be properly seized.

May I use force to effect an arrest and the ensuing search?

You may use only the amount of force necessary, short of deadly force, to accomplish the arrest and the search incident to that arrest.

Is it permissible to search the opposite sex?

The Constitution does not prohibit your searching a member of the opposite sex. Discretion would suggest, however, that whenever possible another officer who is the same sex as the arrestee should conduct the search. You should, of course, do nothing that would be considered "shocking to the conscience" or social norms, to preclude the possibility of suppression of any evidence found during the search or your being held liable individually. In any case, you should follow your agency's guidelines with respect to searching the opposite sex.

41

If I arrest a person in a swimsuit would I still search the person?

Yes, as long as you do not conduct the search in a way that would be shocking to the conscience.

If I arrest a person in the water is there a difference in the search and seizure?

You would be privileged to seize items first and continue the arrest so that you may preserve potential evidence, remove weapons (spear gun, knife, etc.) and bring the subject to a position of safety. As an example, you could motion a diver to the surface, take a spear gun, knife, and carry bag, and then order the diver into a boat and proceed as with any other arrest.

If I arrest heavily clothed suspects such as skiers, ski mobilers, hunters, or ice fishermen, may I search inside their parkas, ski jackets, etc.?

Yes, you may search the individuals regardless of the layers of clothing, and all items within their possession.

B. EXTENT OF SEARCH INCIDENT TO ARREST

Rule of Law: You may search incident to arrest the arrested person and the immediate area around him or her.

What area around the individual am I permitted to search incident to an arrest?

Your search may extend to the area around arrested individuals where they may "jump and reach" a weapon or evidence. As an example, if you arrest a person in a cabin, you may search the area around the chair in which the arrestee is seated or the table in front of him before he rises. You may look in a nearby closet to determine if there is a weapon or the possibility of the destruction of evidence, but this does not include doing a thorough search. Thus, you may not extend the search to other parts or rooms of the cabin, unless you strongly suspect that others are present who may harm you or others or destroy evidence.

Similarly, if you arrest a visitor who is sitting at the picnic table of her rented campsite, you may not search her recreation vehicle or tent incident to the arrest. A warrant should be obtained to extend the search of the premises in which the arrest occurred, unless it is a public area.

C. SEARCH OF POSSESSIONS

What possessions may I search incident to an arrest?

You may search, incident to an arrest, unsealed items within the possession of the arrestee. You may search handbags, briefcases, saddlebags, or similar unlocked items that could hold weapons or evidence. You could also search a rolled up sleeping bag. If you arrest someone in possession of a closed backpack, it may be searched. However, if you take control of the backpack, you would be better off obtaining a warrant before searching it. As an example, you discover two individuals on a blanket who are engaging in the use, sale, or purchase of a half ounce of cocaine. On the blanket is a cooler, a purse, and a backpack. There is also a briefcase which is locked. The individuals' vehicle is parked about 50 feet away from the blanket. Incident to the arrest of the two individuals, you may search their persons, the purse, and the cooler. As for the briefcase, the backpack, and the vehicle, it would be advisable to obtain a warrant to search them.

May I search closed or sealed containers?

If you find any sealed containers in the backpack or cooler, you should obtain a warrant before searching them. Again, you may not search the locked briefcase or the vehicle without first obtaining a search warrant. Because you are responsible for the unprotected property, you should impound the vehicle and perform the necessary *routine* inventory.

Remember, any searches incident to arrest are limited to the time of the arrest, and the privilege vanishes once the arrest is completed and the suspect moved.

D. SEARCH OF VEHICLE INCIDENT TO ARREST

RULE OF LAW: If you arrest an occupant of a vehicle, you may search the interior of the vehicle from which the occupant was removed and any containers therein.

1. **Conventional vehicles**: In addition to searching the interior passenger compartment of the vehicle itself, you may search the trunk or the locked glove compartment if you have reason to believe that they may contain fruits, instrumentalities, or evidence of a crime. Otherwise, you should obtain a search warrant to search or inspect locked or sealed containers found in the vehicle, unless exigent circumstances warrant an immediate search. While there is some support for intrusion into locked or sealed containers without a warrant or exigent circumstances, it is still better to secure such containers and obtain a warrant to open them, *New York v. Belton* notwithstanding.

What is an example of exigent circumstances that would allow such a search without a warrant?

As an example, you may search a locked suitcase if you believe that it contains dangerous items such as explosives, or that the evidence in the suitcase will be destroyed. You may take possession of any locked or sealed items and hold them pending the issuance of a warrant if you proceed deliberately to obtain the warrant and have reason to believe that they contain evidence of a specific crime.

As another example, if you arrest a person from a vehicle in which there is a closed backpack behind the seat, you may

44

search the backpack but you should obtain a warrant to search any sealed containers in the backpack. Unsecured or unsealed containers may be opened in the course of a proper search.

If I arrest a passenger from a vehicle, what is the permissible extent of the vehicle search?

If you arrest a passenger in a vehicle you may search the interior of the vehicle, but not other passengers or their possessions without reasonable cause or exigent circumstances. Similarly, to search the trunk or the locked glove compartment you should have reason to believe that you will find specific evidence relating to the individual arrested.

2. **Recreational vehicles**: Recreational vehicles fall in a unique category of being both vehicle and lodging. The search of the vehicle upon a valid arrest extends to the comparable portion of the RV as it would in a regular vehicle. The passenger compartment may be searched, but the search should not be extended beyond that, without the belief that weapons, evidence or contraband are present and will be destroyed.

The more disabled or stationary the vehicle, the greater the need for a warrant or exigent circumstances. Vehicles, however, may be searched more readily incident to an arrest than other spaces because of their high mobility and their openness to plain view.

What is the permissible extent of a search of a van?

The scope of a search of the interior of a van is similar to that of a conventional vehicle. As a reminder, sealed or locked containers should not normally be searched without a search warrant, exigent circumstances, or strong probable cause.

What is the permissible extent of a search of a motor home?

The interior of a motor home may be searched in a manner similar to that of a conventional vehicle; however, compartments, rooms, and areas closed off from the driving area should not be included in the search incident to arrest without additional probable cause or exigent circumstances. As an example, it would appear that you should not normally search the bathroom incident to an arrest of the driver without exigent circumstances or probable cause requiring such, or unless there is a significant likelihood that the vehicle will be moved.

What is the permissible extent of a search of a slide-in pickup truck camper?

Arrest of an occupant of the pickup does not, in itself, provide a basis for the search of the camper. However, probable cause or exigent circumstances may support the necessity of a search without a warrant.

What is the permissible extent of the search of a recreational vehicle incident to an arrest if the RV is parked?

The more stationary the vehicle, the more it will be treated as a premises and require a search warrant or exigent circumstances. The arrest of an individual in or nearby an RV will allow a search of the individual and the immediate area around the individual, as with any conventional arrest. For example, where a motor home is parked in a campground site and the driver is seated in a chair outside of the vehicle, the search would be of the driver and the immediate area around him. If, instead, he were seated inside his RV, the immediate area around him in the vehicle could be searched.

Are unusual vehicles subject to the same rules of search incident to arrest?

You may, incident to arrest, search all varieties of vehicles, including cycles, snowmobiles, swamp buggies, all-terrain vehicles, etc.

3. **Boats:** You may search incident to an arrest a boat in the same manner that you would search a vehicle. The high mobility and visibility allow this search as is the case in conventional vehicle searches. Accordingly, the larger the vessel the more the search should be confined to the area around the arrestee.

You may search a larger vessel if you have probable cause to believe that it contains evidence that will be destroyed or lost if not seized immediately. The better approach would be to stop and detain the boat and obtain a search warrant as soon as possible.

May I search a swamp buggy, fishing boat, or speed boat pursuant to a stop for operation of the boat in an unsafe manner?

No, not without more. You must effect an arrest of the boat's operator or have probable cause to independently support the search. You may observe all items in plain view and use that observation to support a subsequent arrest or warrant. If you arrest the operator or other occupant, you may search the boat in the same manner as a vehicle. As an example, you may search the tool compartment, ice chest, live well, or similar areas as long as they are not locked. You may not search a motor compartment or similarly removed area unless you have reason to believe that the area contains evidence, fruits, or instrumentalities of the crime.

Incident to the arrest of its operator, may I search a compartmentalized or cabin cruiser?

You may search the area immediately around the operator in the same manner as you would a recreation vehicle. The larger the vessel, the more restricted the area of the search. However, all items observed in plain view may be used to support an arrest or warrant. Likewise, those items may provide probable cause to extend the scope of the search. Obviously, a search warrant should be utilized if possible, and the vessel may be detained for a brief period of time to conduct a necessary investigation or to obtain a search warrant.

When arresting a person in a docked cabin cruiser or houseboat, may I search the vessel?

No. You may search the individual and the area immediately around him or her as in the search of a premises. The vessel should be treated as a premises with mobility and handled accordingly. The more likely that the boat will be moved, the more you may be able to justify a warrantless search. However, a warrant should be obtained whenever possible. You may detain the vessel for a brief period of time to obtain a warrant. Thus, a docked boat should be treated similarly to an RV in a campground.

4. **Aircraft**: The high mobility of aircraft allow them to be treated in the same manner as conventional vehicles. Accordingly, the arrest of the pilot or other occupant will permit a search of the person and the area immediately around him or her. In a small plane this would permit a search of the interior, excluding locked compartments and sealed containers unless exigent circumstances warrant an extension of the search. In a large aircraft you may search in conjunction with the arrest of the pilot the flight deck but you should not extend the search to the aircraft in general without exigent circumstances. As an example, you could search the flight deck, and if you observe what appears to be evidence in the passenger cabin you may seize that evidence under the plain view doctrine. If you have reason to believe that the

airplane contains other evidence, fruits, or instrumentalities of a crime, you may detain the vehicle temporarily to obtain a search warrant. The arrest of crew members or passengers would also permit a search of the immediate area around them.

May I search a helicopter incident to the arrest of the pilot for shooting protected game?

Yes, you may search the helicopter incident to the arrest in the same manner that you could search a conventional vehicle.

When arresting poachers in a campsite, may I search their seaplane tied nearby?

No. Not without other facts creating an immediate need such as a likelihood that the aircraft would be moved and evidence destroyed. Again, you may detain the aircraft and obtain a search warrant.

E. INVENTORIES

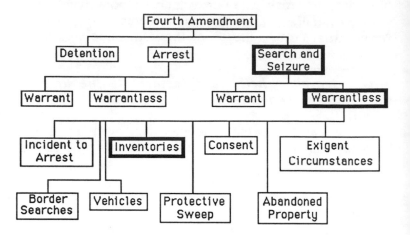

RULE OF LAW: A good-faith routine inventory of personal property is not a search, although evidence, fruits or instrumentalities of a crime discovered incident to the inventory may be seized and properly admitted as evidence. Evidence discovered during the inventory may also be used to support a search warrant. An inventory is NOT a substitute for a search warrant and will be suspect unless it is routine and proper.

You are responsible for property you take or which is left unattended because of an arrest or impoundment removing the operator or owner. Accordingly, you should inventory and secure property left in your control for whatever reason.

What is the extent of an inventory?

Your inventory should be limited to listing in a routine fashion the items you discover. As an example, a sealed envelope should not be opened but listed as a particular item on the inventory. The purpose of an inventory is to protect property and should be carried only as far as necessary for the recording and protection of the property.

May I open containers during my inventory?

Yes, you may open containers in so far as is necessary for identification and accountability of the property. You should not, however, open sealed or locked containers, but mark them for identification.

What are some examples of items that could be opened during an inventory?

You may open any unsealed containers such as: camera cases, pocketbooks, coolers, open envelopes, tobacco cans, film canisters, rifle cases, picnic baskets, beach bags, etc.

You may also open the hood or trunk of a vehicle, or remove the hubcaps and battery and place them in the trunk for safe keeping. However, you should not cause damage to the vehicle (e.g., cut open the seats or door panels).

May I inventory impounded vehicles at random?

No. You should follow a routine inventory procedure. Your department should establish clear written guidelines setting forth the inventory procedures. For example, you should have a routine inventory checklist for vehicles to be used for every impounded, confiscated, or held vehicle.

Is there a difference between inventorying vehicles and other property?

No. The guidelines are essentially the same, and you should follow a routine procedure for inventorying any property that comes into your possession. For example, you could inventory the contents of an arrested visitor's backpack, provided that you do not break any sealed containers. You may, however, seize any evidence, fruits or instrumentalities of a crime discovered in the course of a proper inventory.

Should my agency have a written inventory procedure?

Yes. The Court has consistently reaffirmed the importance of a written inventory policy that is strictly followed. An example of a model inventory policy is provided as a guide in Chapter XIV of this book.

What if, during an inventory, I find evidence of a crime?

To insure that any further evidence is admissible, it would be wise to stop the inventory immediately, secure the property, and seek a search warrant for the vehicle/property.

F. SEARCH INCIDENT TO A CITATION

Do I have the authority to search a visitor incident to writing him a citation?

No. You may **NOT** search the person of an individual to whom you have issued a citation or court summons, if you do not plan to take that person into physical custody. However, if you believe the individual to be armed and dangerous, you may frisk him or her for weapons.

Do I have the authority to search the area around a visitor to whom I have written a citation?

No. The issuance of a citation or summons does NOT as a rule justify a search of the area around the person being issued the citation or summons. For example, if you observe a visitor smoking marijuana in a vehicle in a parking lot, and you confiscate the cigarette and issue a citation, you are not justified in searching the vehicle, hoping to find a "baggie" of marijuana. However, state law and park regulations may vary on this issue, and you are encouraged to become familiar with the particular guidelines under which you must operate.

NOTES

CHAPTER VII

SEARCH AND SEIZURE

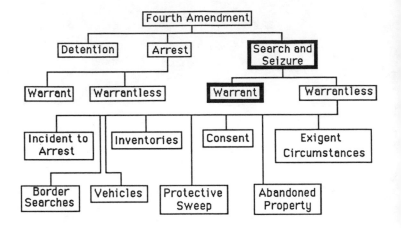

A. SEARCHES WITH A WARRANT

If you have probable cause to believe that contraband or evidence of a crime is in a particular location, you may present under oath or affirmation the facts or apparent facts before a judge or magistrate and request that a search warrant be issued. In order to obtain a search warrant, you will also have to specify (1) the object or objects to be seized and (2) the particular location where the object(s) are to be found.

Because of the "warrant requirement" of the Fourth Amendment, it is generally good policy to obtain a warrant before searching anyone's private property. Failure to obtain a warrant prior to a search may result in the inadmissibility of that evidence in court, and could expose you to liability. Currently, the courts appear to be moving in the direction of increased reliance on search warrants.

What is a search warrant?

A warrant is an order from the issuing court directing an officer or class of officers (e.g., any National Park ranger) to carry out a particular action, such as conduct a search for illegal drugs or related paraphernalia.

From whom may I obtain a search warrant?

Like arrest warrants, search warrants may be obtained by appearing before any judge, magistrate, or justice of the peace, regardless of jurisdiction. However, it is advisable to seek an arrest warrant from the judge or magistrate associated with your particular jurisdiction. Federal warrants normally require the judge or magistrate to be of a court of record (i.e., as opposed to a justice of the peace).

What kinds of information may I use to establish probable cause for a search warrant?

You may use personal knowledge or observation, or information obtained from a reliable source that you believe to be accurate. The accuracy may be determined by your observation of events following the report of the informant. For example, a camper approaches you and tells you that another camper appears to be selling drugs from a tent. You observe the second camper handing something to another person. You may seek a search warrant for the tent, based on your informant's report and your observation.

May I obtain a search warrant by providing a judge with the necessary information over the telephone?

Although some jurisdictions may apply other restrictions, case and statutory law today generally allows telephonic warrants for circumstances in which it is impossible or impractical for you to physically appear before a judge or magistrate first. Of course, such warrant applications must eventually be supported by the same evidence or affidavit as any other warrant. The telephonic warrant should be used for urgent situations, not merely inconvenient ones.

What are the restrictions on a search with a warrant?

There are seven basic restrictions:

1. A member of the class of officers, although he or she may be assisted by other officers, to whom the warrant is directed must be present at the search and should generally be the first to initiate execution (entry, etc.). As an example, a warrant directed to a U.S. Fish and Wildlife officer to search a cabin and the adjoining buildings for poached Bald Eagle carcasses or evidence thereof should be carried out by at least one Fish and Wildlife officer, but he or she may be assisted by others, for example park rangers, sheriff deputies, drug agents, etc.

2. The search warrant must be executed within a reasonable time period after its issuance. As a general rule, a week should be an adequate time to complete the execution of the warrant. Local rules will dictate the time of return of the warrant. If your warrant is not executed in a timely manner, a new warrant may be necessary. It is not uncommon for new evidence to be required to obtain a new warrant to replace a warrant not executed in a timely manner.

3. The search must take place in the particular location directed by the warrant. For example, a warrant to search for stolen park equipment in a house may be extended to those buildings that are in close proximity to the house. A warrant to search the barn for a stolen park tractor, however, would not extend to other buildings, including the house.

4. The search must be for the particular item(s) specified in the warrant, and you may search only in places where the item(s) could reasonably be located. If you have a warrant for narcotics, you could look in all places where

narcotics may be hidden, such as a refrigerator, medicine cabinet, closet, or drawers. If, on the other hand, you are searching for the remains of a poached bear, you could search only where a bear could be, such as the freezer. You could not, of course, search for the bear in a medicine cabinet. See "Elephant Rule" in the glossary.

5. The warrant, with the list of items seized and all appropriate inventories, must be returned to the court, within the prescribed or a reasonable time. If the warrant is not returned in a timely manner the officer must be prepared to explain the delay or face possible loss of the evidence.

6. A warrant issued is normally valid for the daytime unless night searches are specified or the statutory laws of the jurisdiction permit nighttime searches. A warrant for the daytime may, however, be started in the day and continued into the night if done in a consistent and deliberate manner and if it is not done for harassment.

7. A search warrant is valid only for a single search expedition. If the need arises for a return to the premises a new warrant should be obtained.

If I am executing a search warrant for stolen park signs, and I find narcotics in a medicine cabinet and a stolen park chain saw in the garage, may I seize them and use them as evidence?

You may use the stolen chain saw as evidence because it was found in a location where signs could be hidden. The narcotics, on the other hand, should be inadmissible because they were found in a location outside of the scope of the warrant. See "Elephant Rule."

While conducting a premises search pursuant to a search warrant, may I search any individuals present?

You may always perform a "Terry" frisk if you have reason to believe that the individuals are armed and dangerous, and you may prevent any individuals from interfering with the search. However, you may search these individuals only on the basis of probable cause that they have in their possession objects that are the target of the search or, based on circumstances present, that they have on their person evidence or contraband of a particular crime.

What are the jurisdictional restrictions on executing search warrants?

If you are within your park boundary or within another park in your jurisdiction, you may:

1. execute a search warrant issued for your jurisdiction and related to criminal activity in your park system.

2. execute a search warrant issued for your jurisdiction but not related to criminal activity in your park system.

If you are outside your park boundary but within your state you may:

1. execute a search warrant issued for your jurisdiction and for criminal conduct related to your scope of activity. If you are a local park ranger, other restrictions may apply.

2. assist other officers in the execution of their search warrants.

If you are outside your park boundary and outside your state you may:

1. not execute any search warrants unless you are a federal officer.

2. assist other officers in the execution of their warrants.

B. SEARCHES WITHOUT A WARRANT

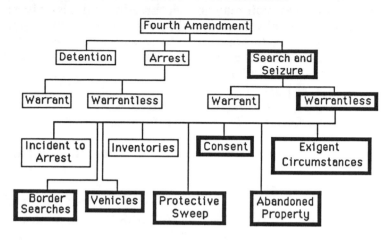

Are there any exceptions to the warrant requirement for a search?

Yes. Legal tradition has created eight exceptions to the warrant requirement for a search:

1. **Searches incident to arrest**: These searches were discussed in Chapter VI of this book. They are limited in scope, and in general they would not include locked or sealed containers.

2. **Inventories**: The purpose of an inventory is to secure property left in your control for whatever reason. Inventories were also discussed in Chapter VI of this book.

3. **Consent searches**: These searches are generally difficult to uphold in court unless you obtain a valid consent and should be used only as a last resort. In order for the consent to be valid, it must be made in the absence of duress or intimidation, a condition not typical of most people under arrest. It is a good idea to inform an individual from whom you want consent for a search that he or she is free to deny consent. Once consent is given, the party is free to ask the officers to discontinue the search at any time.

If you are asked to stop the consent search, you should do so. However, all evidence seized up to that point may be used in court or to obtain a search warrant for continuation of the search. If you have probable cause, you may secure the premises, vehicle, or possessions to obtain a warrant and continue the search, provided you move to obtain the warrant as soon as possible.

Who may legitimately consent to a search?

In order for persons to give consent to a search, they must appear to have a legitimate control over the area or things to be searched. For example, consider the following situations:

a. The owner or operator of a motor home could consent to have it searched for drugs that his son may be selling.

b. The renter of a campsite could consent to have her tent searched for the fruits of a burglary that her friend may have committed.

c. The manager of the park inn could consent to the search of a guest's room if it is past checkout time, and the guest had not paid for the following evening, unless standard procedures were simply to allow the guest to stay over and settle the bill at the end. If later settlement is allowed then in order for the consent search to be justified, the abandonment must be apparent, such as the guest not being in the room for a day or two, removing all the luggage, loading it, driving away, etc. The abandonment of the premises should be evident, either actual or apparent. A brief time after the checkout time may not be abandonment but a substantial time, several hours or actual departure, probably would be.

d. The manager of a campground could consent to the search of an abandoned tent site or parking area. In general, the guidelines in (d) above would also apply.

e. The manager of the park inn could <u>not</u> consent to the search of a guest's room in which the guest was legitimately registered.

f. A roommate in the dorm where seasonal park employees are housed could <u>not</u> consent to a search of her roommate's belongings. The roommate could, however, consent to a search of the jointly-occupied premises, and plain view discoveries may lead to a search of the personal belongings of the roommate. A search warrant is, of course, better to preserve the use of evidence. As an example, a warrant may be obtained on the basis of plain-view discovery so that the subsequent search is protected. The premises could be secured for a reasonable time (overnight) to prevent the removal or destruction of evidence.

g. The manager of recreation facilities could <u>not</u> normally consent to a search of a locker legitimately rented by a third party, until it is abandoned or the leased time has lapsed.

h. A hiker could <u>not</u> consent to the search of his or her friend's backpack.

Does consent to search a vehicle extend to closed containers found inside the vehicle?

It is reasonable to consider the suspect's consent to include examination of unlocked, unsealed containers that may reasonably contain the object of the search. There must be specific consent for the search of any sealed or locked containers, and a suspect may limit the scope of the search at any time.

4. **Exigent (emergency) circumstances**: If it is a true emergency and you are unable to take the time to obtain a search warrant, you may conduct a warrantless search. For example, you may hear screams coming from inside a motor home in the campground or from a cabin rented to visitors. You may see what appears to be blood dripping from the

trunk of a car, or you may have reason to believe that a bomb has been placed in some location that is privately controlled. You may believe that if you take time to obtain a warrant, the evidence will be destroyed or removed, or you may believe that someone's life may be in danger.

5. The vehicle exception:

a. **Automobiles**: The openness and mobility of vehicles allow you to search them more readily than other areas. As a general rule, vehicle searches may be conducted if you have reason to believe that the vehicle contains specific evidence of a crime and that a delay in obtaining a warrant will result in the loss of the evidence. You may, of course, secure the vehicle and proceed immediately to obtain a warrant. You may use plain-view observation of the interior and exterior to support a warrant. As an example, you observe what you believe to be a "baggie" of marijuana on the floor of the van. You could secure the vehicle and seek a warrant, or if you believe that it will be moved and the evidence destroyed you may proceed to seize the evidence.

The difficulty in searching a vehicle not incident to arrest and without a warrant is that you run the risk of not being able to persuade the court that your action was the only alternative and that the need was sufficient to proceed without a warrant.

b. **Boats**: Because of their mobility and visibility, boats are to be treated similarly to conventional vehicles in that the expectation of privacy is reduced. Vessels of the cabin variety should be treated as RVs or premises, as appropriate.

Boats may be boarded for safety inspections more readily than vehicles, due to the necessity of checking safety equipment such as fire extinguishers and life preservers. Any evidence observed in plain view may be seized and used to support an arrest or warrant. Obviously boats may be stopped for unsafe or reckless operation, for lack of running lights, etc.

Boats may also be stopped to inspect an operator's fishing or hunting license, fish or game limits, or boat registration or area permit. Furthermore, such inspections may be made on a random basis, as long as they are not made in a discriminatory fashion. Evidence observed in plain view may be seized and used to support an arrest or warrant.

c. **Aircraft**: Aircraft should be treated in the same manner as boats and conventional vehicles. As with boats, airplanes may be boarded for safety inspections, and evidence observed in plain view may be seized and used to support an arrest or warrant.

An aircraft may be boarded without a warrant if there are exigent circumstances or probable cause that it contains evidence of a crime or violations of hunting or fishing limits.

6. **Protective sweeps**: Where there is a legitimate need to secure an area for such purposes as: public safety (e.g., bomb threat), dignitary protection, protection of officers conducting searches, prevention of the destruction of evidence, etc., you may perform a protective sweep of the area. Evidence discovered during the course of a proper sweep can be seized.

7. **Abandoned property**: Property that has been discarded may be searched without a warrant. This would include such things as: any property that is discarded by a suspect attempting to avoid discovery by law enforcement officers, thrown out the window of a vehicle or a cabin, left unattended in a public area for an extended period of time, remaining in a hotel room after a person has checked out, etc.

Additionally, garbage placed for collection or discard at the point where the public or animals would have access to it is generally considered abandoned. For example, items in a garbage can by a rented tent site could be searched without a warrant. Likewise, a garbage bag left for collection or discarded in the bushes could also be searched.

8. Border searches: Individuals attempting to enter the United States are subject to a complete search of their person and all property in their possession.

NOTES

CHAPTER VIII

SUSPECT IDENTIFICATION

RULE OF LAW: A witness identification of a suspect will generally be admissible in court so long as the identification procedure is not unduly suggestive.

Suspect identification by a witness may be accomplished by single identification, photographic identification, and lineup identification. In each of the situations care must be taken to avoid unnecessary suggestibility as to a particular accused. Timeliness is also an important factor.

A. SINGLE IDENTIFICATION

Single identification occurs when you apprehend a suspect shortly after and in the vicinity of a crime and return that suspect to the victim/witness for identification. The logic of the court is that you are as likely to free the innocent as identify the guilty. The procedure should be accomplished with the least possible delay, and there should be no suggestion or influence by the officer.

How much delay is permissible in a single identification?

The time should be measured in minutes and not hours. As an example, a visitor reports seeing someone break into a car in a parking lot. Twenty minutes later you apprehend a person matching the description. You may take that person back to the visitor for identification. If, however, the person is apprehended several hours later, such an identification would be inappropriate; rather, identification should be made through a photographic or physical lineup.

*What if the suspect insists on an immediate iden-
tification?*

Regardless of the time frame, if an apprehended suspect insists on being returned for immediate identification by a vic-
tim/witness, you may conduct such an identification or hold
the suspect for a conventional lineup as soon as possible.

*Suppose the identification cannot be made until
later because the witness is being treated in a hospital. May a single identification still be made?*

Yes. Because you are as likely to free the innocent as identify the guilty, you may use the bedside identification if such
proves necessary because of the witness' condition or other
exigent circumstances. A photographic identification may
also be employed under these circumstances.

*May the witness be asked if this is the person who
committed the offense?*

Yes. You may ask, "Is this the person who committed the
offense?" You would be wise to precede the question with
the statement that all persons closely matching the description are being brought in for identification.

B. Photographic Lineups

Under conditions when a physical lineup is not feasible or
appropriate, a witness may be asked to identify a suspect
from a group of photographs. As with any general lineup
procedure, the pictures should not be presented in any suggestive manner, sequence, or pattern. Furthermore, the
photographs of the non-suspects should match the general
appearance of the suspect.

*How many pictures should be in a photographic
lineup?*

Obviously, the more pictures of different individuals shown
to the witness, the more likely the identification will be free
from taint. As an example, a photographic lineup that in-

cludes the suspect and three or four pictures of other individuals would be sufficient. The aim is to require the witness to independently undergo a non-suggestive decision-making process.

Can a single picture be used in a photographic lineup?

Yes. A single picture may be used under some circumstances, such as following an armed robbery where the suspect is known, the modus operandi (M.O.), is similar, and the suspect is armed and dangerous. The application of rules of exigency are wise here, and you are always better off using more than one photograph to avoid the taint of suggestibility.

C. CONVENTIONAL LINEUPS

A conventional lineup is one conducted of several individuals, one of whom is the suspect. The lineup should always include individuals of the same race and sex and of similar build and characteristics. For example, a suspect of medium build and height, with a beard, should be placed in a lineup with other persons also of a similar build, with a beard, and all with close hair color.

If my suspect is six feet tall, must all of the persons in the lineup be six feet tall?

The suspect must not stand out as the only person six feet tall, if such is a factor, but you may have others of similar size, give or take approximately two inches.

If my suspect has dark skin, must all others be of the same tone?

The tone should be as close as possible but does not have to match exactly. As an example, a light skinned person of a dark race may be included with a tanned person if other characteristics are satisfactory.

What should I do if I cannot find but one other person of similar description?

This would be an ideal time to use a photographic lineup of the suspect and others, using mug shots. If the time frame is short enough a single identification may be appropriate. Otherwise, forego the lineup at this stage and secure a good written description. Do take a photograph of the suspect to be placed with others at a later time. If the matter is of sufficient importance, remember that the witness can be held or delayed a reasonable time. The witness could become hostile, however, so you must use discretion in such situations.

How many persons other than the suspect need I have in a lineup?

Obviously the more the better, but three or four more than the suspect is probably adequate.

Does a suspect have a right to have his or her lawyer present during a physical lineup?

Yes. Unlike the single identification and the photographic lineup, a suspect has a right to a lawyer present during a physical lineup, if the individual has been formally charged. It is wise to provide the opportunity for counsel if the person is the principle suspect.

NOTES

CHAPTER IX

EVIDENCE

A. DEFINITION

Evidence is any form of proof, or probative matter, legally presented at a trial by the parties through the use of witnesses, records, documents, and concrete objects for the purpose of inducing belief in the minds of the court or jury. Evidence includes the presentation of any facts in a case that tend to either confirm or deny the truth of an assertion made by one of the parties in the case.

What types of evidence are there?

Evidence may be either *direct* or *circumstantial*.

Direct evidence is any evidence that, in and of itself, tends to confirm an element or issue in question in the trial, without the need to produce other facts necessary to its introduction. An example would be eye witness testimony.

Circumstantial evidence is indirect evidence; that is, it involves facts from which the truth of an issue may be logically inferred. An example would be fingerprints on the murder weapon or testimony from a witness that he was in the area at the time the shot was heard and saw the defendant near the scene at about the time of the offense.

What are the different categories of evidence?

Evidence may be **testimonial**; that is, provided in the form of a testimony by a person, such as an eye witness or a person giving a confession.

Evidence may be **documentary**; that is, every form of writing, such as the guest register of the park inn or a concessioner's financial records.

Evidence may be **real;** that is, all items directly involved in the incident such as blood stains, tire marks, powder burns, or a gun.

Demonstrative evidence is normally relevant and admissible if it demonstrates that the crime was committed and sheds some light on how it was committed. It includes weapons, blood-stained clothing, lifted fingerprints, photographs, mock-ups, models and similar items to aid in understanding the testimony.

Normally the conclusions or opinions of a witness are irrelevant and accordingly inadmissible. Qualified witnesses may render estimates or opinions of sobriety, age, race, speed, etc. Experts may testify and give professional opinions only in the area of their expertise, but they may not testify about common matters.

B. ADMISSIBILITY OF EVIDENCE

What is required to get evidence admitted at trial?

1. The evidence must be **relevant**; it must have some bearing on the facts at issue in the case. The question to ask is, does the evidence tend to prove or disprove the guilt of a person charged with a crime? As an example, evidence showing that a defendant owned a large mixed ring of General Motors keys might be relevant if the accused is charged with illegally entering General Motors vehicles in the park and taking property from them.

2. The evidence must be **trustworthy**; it must be demonstrated that the evidence was not altered or tampered with. The *chain of custody* is an important means of preserving the integrity of the evidence as it is transferred from one person to another.

3. The evidence must be **competent**; that is, it must have been obtained within the constitutional guidelines (most often the Fourth and Fifth Amendments), or it may be subject to suppression under the *Exclusionary Rule.*

Under what conditions may I legally obtain physical or documentary evidence of a crime?

1. If you observe it in plain view when you had a legitimate right to be where you were when you saw it.

2. If you have a valid warrant to search for it.

3. If you have a valid consent to search for it.

4. If you discover it during a search incident to a valid arrest.

5. If someone willingly gives it to you.

6. If you discover it on public or in abandoned property.

7. If you find abandoned property that itself becomes evidence.

8. If you discover it during a valid inventory of a vehicle or other item.

9. If you inadvertently discover it during the course of a proper "Terry" frisk.

C. CHAIN OF CUSTODY

How do I protect the chain of custody?

To demonstrate the trustworthiness of any evidence you must be able to do the following two things:

1. account for and document its whereabouts from the time you discovered it until it is entered at trial.

2. detail who had access to it from the time you discovered it until it is entered at trial.

For example, you seize a pound of marijuana that you discover in a vehicle you were searching incident to the arrest of its driver for selling drugs in a campground. You place the evidence in a sealed container and tag it with information regarding when, where, and from whom it was seized and who seized it. You then turn the evidence over to someone who is in charge of the locked property room, safe, or other system for storing evidence in a secure manner. Furthermore, you document the transfer on paper.

Similarly, any time the evidence is moved or changes hands it should be documented in writing, until it is finally admitted at trial. At no point in its "chain" should there be a possibility of tampering with or altering the evidence.

What if I intend to send evidence through the mail?

Any evidence sent through the mail should be sent "registered" which means that it travels in a locked pouch that must be signed for upon delivery. For example, you arrest a person for driving while intoxicated on a road in the wildlife refuge. He submits to a blood alcohol test at the local hospital. At the hospital you witness the drawing of the sample, seal the container and mail it to a forensic laboratory for analysis. The package should be sent by "registered" mail. Unless the laboratory is familiar with procedures for handling evidence, you should request that it be returned by registered mail.

D. RULES OF EVIDENCE

What are the Rules of Evidence?

Both the federal and state court systems have written rules or guidelines that establish the admissibility of evidence at trial. These rules are actually rules of process or exclusion; they elaborate what will be acceptable and unacceptable as evidence, and how the evidence should be offered.

What are some examples of rules of evidence?

1. **Best Evidence Rule**: This rule requires that the most reliable proof of a fact be utilized. As an example, the original written document is best evidence, not a copy or

photocopy. Thus, the park inn's guest register is admitted to show that a particular person signed it, whereas a photocopy would be admitted only if the original register were lost, destroyed, or completely unusable or is unavailable.

2. **Hearsay Rule**: Hearsay evidence is what a witness heard another person say and is generally inadmissible to prove the truth of a fact at issue. It may be admissible under some circumstances, such as a dying declaration, or an admission against interest of the declarant. As an example, one camper testifies that another camper said that he had bought narcotics from the campground attendant. This would be inadmissible as hearsay; however, it might be used to support a warrant. If, on the other hand, one camper testified that she used narcotics with another camper who said he bought them from the attendant, it is probably admissible because it represents a statement against her own interest.

E. ADMISSIONS AND CONFESSIONS

An **admission** is normally less than a confession, but it is a statement against personal interest. Guilt may be inferred from an admission that acknowledges facts which, when combined with other facts, will produce such a conclusion.

A **confession** is the total acknowledgement of the accused that he or she is guilty of the offense charged.

F. THE EXCLUSIONARY RULE

The **exclusionary rule** is an artificial rule created by the courts that allows the court or defendant to suppress valid evidence for trial purposes if it was illegally obtained by officers or agents of the government acting under color of law. The evidence may be admissible for other purposes, such as Grand Jury evidence, preliminary hearings, impeachment of witnesses not telling the truth on the stand in the trial, etc.

Normally a motion to suppress evidence will be heard at a pre-trial hearing and, in some instances, in the trial process itself. The officer obtaining the evidence will normally be called to support its use, and any other persons will be heard to support or deny its use. The judge will make the decision to suppress or admit the evidence, and he or she may do so at the hearing, shortly after it, or take the matter under advisement for a ruling at a later time. It is also possible that the "taint" may be purged by eventual discovery or some other curative action.

What does it mean to "purge the taint"?

Although evidence may be suppressible because of the way it was collected (seized), the "taint" created by the officer's action might be cured by other existing circumstances. As an example, eventual discovery, standing, or the existence of other relevant evidence may permit the use of the evidence in some form. In other words, if the use of evidence is blocked because of some constitutional violation, there is a possibility that it might be admitted through some other avenue.

What is standing?

Standing refers to the right of a person to contest the admissibility of evidence because his or her individual constitutional rights were violated. As an example, you have no right (standing) to complain about a constitutional violation if you are not an injured party. Standing is frequently determined by possession or ownership.

Should I destroy or release evidence that was seized under questionable circumstances?

No. Because of the possibility of purging the taint, the evidence may not be suppressed by the court, and even if it is it may be valuable at trial to impeach a witness not telling the truth. The evidence may also be used in Grand Jury hearings and preliminary hearings unless prohibited by law.

Should I try to make evidence that I have obtained conform to the desires of the court in order to preserve it?

Not as stated, but you should make your actions and procedures conform to good constitutional standards so that you have protected evidence and can rely on good faith in your actions. You should, of course, protect evidence so that the chain of custody is followed and the evidence is preserved.

To what does the fruit of the "poisonous tree" refer?

Otherwise legal and proper evidence obtained as the product of other illegal police activity may not, as a rule, be admitted at trial. You should always check with the prosecutor's office if you have questions regarding the propriety of any evidence in your possession.

NOTES

CHAPTER X

TALKING WITH SUSPECTS

A. CONVENTIONAL CONVERSATION

Unlike most police officers, park rangers are not really "out of place" if they want to engage a visitor in general conversation in most park environments. Because of their role as stewards of the park, it would not be considered inappropriate for rangers, for example, to casually approach some visitors on a trail or in a campground and make "small talk" with them, to ask them if they are enjoying their visit, etc. Nor would it be inappropriate after dark to approach a visitor and ask him if everything is alright or if he saw illegal activity, damage to the park, illegal camping, drinking, etc. Such intrusions would not generally be considered unreasonable as long as they do not interfere with the visitor's enjoyment of the park and are not intruding unnecessarily into the visitor's privacy.

Of course, this latitude given to you as a park law enforcement officer works to your advantage when you are suspicious that criminal activity may be present. Because you may make such contacts legitimately, anything you may observe, hear, or smell of an illegal nature during such a contact would serve to help develop probable cause for further legal action. For example, you approach a parked car in the park at 3:00 AM to inquire whether the occupants are in need of assistance, and you see a "baggie" of what appears to be marijuana in plain view in the ashtray. You could confiscate the baggie and write a citation or make an arrest for the controlled substance.

Remember, in these situations of conventional conversation, park visitors are under no obligation to talk to you. Good faith on your part is an important factor. There is an exception to the rule, however, where your interest is created by constructive consent because of a hunting or fishing license or back country permit. See "Administrative Contacts" below.

B. Administrative Contacts

In order to conduct park administrative tasks, rangers and park police also have the right to initiate contacts with visitors when appropriate. Examples of such contacts would include: checks for fishing licenses, boating permits, camping registrations, back country hiking permits, etc. If, during such a contact, you detect illegal activity, you could pursue it further. For example, you approach a fisherman to check his license and, upon contacting him, notice that the fisherman is using illegal bait. Your discovery would provide a legal basis for a citation or arrest. Or, you approach a tent in a campground to collect the registration fee from its occupant. While standing by the tent you observe in the tent several backpacks that match the description of ones that had been stolen earlier that day. You may seize the backpacks and arrest the occupant of the tent site.

As in the case of conventional conversation, park visitors are under no legal obligation to answer your questions in these administrative situations. Their failure to do so, however, would typically mean that they are violating some law, rule or regulation that would allow you to take further action. For example, a ranger approaches a fishing visitor and asks to see her fishing license, but she refuses to produce one. Such an action on her part could, of course, lead to a citation or arrest.

C. Investigative Contacts

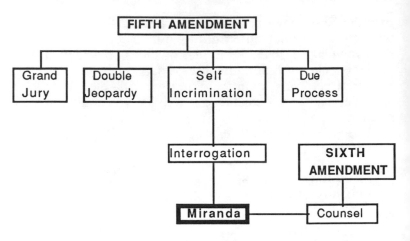

If you have reason to believe that a crime may have occurred and you are investigating the incident further, you have a right to ask questions of people whom you reasonably feel may have some knowledge of the incident. These people fall into two categories: (a) those who may have some information about the incident but are not suspects, and (b) those who may have some knowledge about the incident because they are suspects or potential suspects.

Furthermore, in this second group there are two subcategories: (1) those whom you have no intention of taking into physical custody and (2) those whom you may take into custody. It is important to remember that NO ONE in any of the above categories is under any legal obligation to tell you ANYTHING.

If you plan to question a suspect it is always wise to provide him or her with the "Miranda" warnings. It is **necessary** to provide the suspect with "Miranda" warnings if you take him or her into custody and are going to interrogate that person.

What rights are included in the Miranda warnings?

The suspect must be advised of the following:

1. You have a right to remain silent.

2. Anything you say can be used against you in a court of law.

3. You have a right to have a lawyer, either of your own choice or court appointed, if you cannot afford one.

4. You have a right to talk to your lawyer before answering any questions and to have him or her present during any questioning, if you wish.

When must I read the Miranda rights to a suspect?

While actually reading the Miranda warnings may be best for accuracy or procedure, you may just state them if you are confident that you can repeat the content accurately. Miranda warnings must be provided before questioning anyone whom you intend to take into physical custody (i.e., arrest). Also, it is an excellent idea to inform people of their Miranda rights in the following circumstances:

1. if you ask a person to accompany you to headquarters or to the ranger office or to another police department for questioning;

2. before you question a person whom you have placed in your patrol car, patrol boat, etc;

3. before you question a suspect to whom the Miranda warnings have not been read for several hours; or if you are unaware that they have been given recently;

4. before you question a suspect after someone else has read him or her the Miranda warnings during a prior questioning;

5. if you had to use physical force to gain a person's compliance for a frisk, arrest, or search.

After waiving Miranda rights and answering some questions, may a suspect refuse to answer any further questions?

Yes. If a suspect waives Miranda rights and agrees to answer your questions, he or she still has the right to stop answering questions at any point during the interrogation.

It is important to remember that in any subsequent proceedings it will be your responsibility to prove waiver.

After waiving his Miranda rights, a suspect decides to talk to me. If his or her attorney is waiting to speak to him or her, do I have to inform the suspect?

No. Although it may be a better procedure to so inform the suspect, it is not necessary. The privilege of asking for the advice of an attorney accrues to the suspect and not the attorney.

Before informing a suspect of his or her Miranda rights, do I have to disclose the subject matter of the intended interrogation?

No. The important thing is to insure that the suspect is aware of his or her rights so he or she may request assistance of counsel or elect to remain silent.

May I reinitiate interrogation without counsel present after the suspect has requested and been provided counsel?

No. You may not reinitiate interrogation without counsel present after the accused has requested and been provided counsel. The Fifth Amendment protection is not terminated or suspended after the suspect has consulted with an attorney. Before reinitiating interrogation, you should consult with the suspect's counsel.

As a reminder - - - You are the one who will have to convince the court that you have provided the warnings by your actions, procedures, obvious good faith actions, etc.

D. TALKING WITH FOREIGN NATIONALS

If you have a law enforcement encounter with a foreign national with whom you have difficulty communicating, you should obtain a translator or forego questioning. Notify your supervisor and the nearest appropriate prosecutor's office if you take the individual into custody. Be calm, careful, and proceed with caution, but be firm.

E. TALKING WITH PERSONS WITH SPEECH OR HEARING PROBLEMS

If you have a law enforcement encounter with a person with speech or hearing difficulties, you should obtain a person who can sign or respond appropriately. If you cannot do so, forego questioning. If you effect an arrest, notify your supervisor, the nearest office that can provide assistance to the handicapped person, and the nearest appropriate prosecutor's office. Be calm, careful, and proceed with caution, but be firm.

NOTES

CHAPTER XI

SURVEILLANCE

A. SURVEILLANCE BY OFFICERS

You may observe anything from a place you have a right to be. You may use any device to aid your visual surveillance such as binoculars, a telescope, infrared devices, etc. You should not use observable devices such as a flashlight because the observation process should not obviously intrude into privacy. The key to proper surveillance is to remember that the visitor has a **reasonable expectation of privacy** and you may intrude only when you have a real need for the information. If electronic surveillance is utilized, you should be prepared to show that this is the only way or only safe way the information can be obtained.

Surveillance may be conducted from another vehicle, from a tree, an aircraft, a boat, an adjoining campsite, etc. Anything you observe during your surveillance may be used as evidence or to support an arrest or search warrant.

What is a curtilage?

A **curtilage** is a dwelling and the immediate area around it in which there is a reasonable expectation of privacy acceptable to society. A dwelling is a place where people reside and has been set aside for their exclusive use. Dwellings include: homes, condominiums, apartments, rented rooms, cabins, mobile home sites, and any out buildings within a reasonable proximity that have been set aside for that exclusive use. The concept of curtilage may also include areas set aside for extended personal use, such as trailer or tent sites in camp grounds.

What is the extent of a curtilage?

The curtilage includes the special area of family privacy within the "picket fence." It does not include buildings some distance from the home, areas across a public road, or places of business.

What are the relevant rules regarding surveillance with respect to a curtilage?

You have a right to engage in surveillance of a curtilage so long as you are not on the curtilage and do not intrude onto it. As an example, you may observe from the public road, from an open field, from outside the fence, from an adjacent building, or from an aircraft. You may not encroach by physical intrusion onto the curtilage itself. Specifically, as part of a poaching investigation, you could not sneak up to a suspect's house or cabin and peer in the window looking for poached animals.

May I approach and peer in the window of a motor home that is parked on a site in the campground and being used as a temporary dwelling?

Without further facts, you probably should not because a reasonable expectation of privacy exists.

May I approach and peer in the window of a motor home that is parked in the Visitor Center parking lot?

Yes, you may, even if it appears as though it is illegally parked there over night. In this situation the reasonable expectation of privacy is reduced.

May I use binoculars, night scopes or bionic ears to observe activity within a curtilage as long as I don't physically intrude onto it?

Yes, you may use binoculars or night scopes. However, if your surveillance is to involve electronic listening devices, you should obtain the necessary warrant because of the planned nature of the intrusion. Plain hearing or listening does not require a warrant and may be used as evidence or to support an arrest or a warrant.

The courts seem to be moving toward allowing the enhancement of vision from your own non-intrusive position. Heat sensors and light enhancement devices would seem to be permissible. Sound enhancement, however, must not fall into the electronic eavesdropping category (for which you need a warrant).

May I set up a tent from which to observe activity in adjoining campsites?

Yes. You may observe all activity you can see (including use of binoculars or scopes) and use the observation to support a warrant or effect an arrest. You may use a recording device (e.g., recording from the tent) to record any overheard remarks to support a warrant or effect an arrest.

May I use a boat in dock to observe activity?

Yes. You may observe all activity and listen unaided to the conversations. You may record, unaided, from the boat all that you hear.

May I wire another person and record the conversations in which he or she engages?

Yes. You may use recording or transmitting devices placed on another person to transmit all conversations of people talking with the wired individual. The court will allow this as being more accurate than testimony of the wired person. You may not, however, place a microphone near a campsite, vehicle, phone booth, etc. without the necessary warrant. You could, however, set up a recording device in a site nearby and record all sounds naturally coming to the site.

May I listen in on an extension phone to a conversation?

Yes. You may listen if you have the consent of any of the parties in the conversation. If you do not have the consent of at least one of the parties, you may not listen in without a warrant.

Do I need a warrant to listen to conversations in a cabin?

You should have a warrant to listen to sounds since the occupants have a reasonable expectation of privacy. You may observe from a public or adjoining area all activity around you and use that or any sounds heard by the unaided ear to support an arrest or warrant.

What if I hear a scream or shot?

You may respond as in any exigent circumstance and enter the premises to insure the safety of others.

Where do I get the sound surveillance warrant?

You should contact your prosecutor to assist you in obtaining the warrant.

B. INFORMANTS

Informants may be used to support search or arrest warrants and, under appropriate circumstances, warrantless arrests. You may stop individuals pursuant to an informant's information to determine the presence of criminal activity.

Informants should be reliable; that is, the information, coupled with past reliability of the informant or other corroborating circumstances, would lead a reasonable ranger acting in good faith to believe that sufficient probable cause exists to proceed with an arrest or seek a warrant.

If, for example, a park visitor tells me that the individual in the next vehicle or boat has a weapon in his waistband and is selling cocaine from his cooler what may I do?

You may **stop** the individual, reach into the waistband (frisk), take the weapon, and, based on that (corroboration), open the cooler and effect the arrest.

C. Open Fields

Open fields are the areas outside of occupied premises, and the area immediately around such, including most park areas and public space, where a ranger may go freely. You may observe and listen from these areas and use such observations to effect an arrest or support a warrant.

D. Plain View

Any evidence, fruits, or instrumentalities of a crime that you observe without your having to move anything, turn anything over, or open anything up may be seized. This "plain view" doctrine requires that (1) you have a legal right to be where you were when you saw the evidence, and (2) you did not have to move or manipulate anything to make the evidence observable. In such cases a "search" has not taken place.

If I see a shotgun at a person's camp site and want to check it to see if it is stolen, may I turn it over to read the serial number?

No. Assuming that a shotgun is not illegal to possess, turning the weapon over to read the serial number would be considered a search and would not come under the "plain view" doctrine.

NOTES

CHAPTER XII

ENTRAPMENT

A. DEFINITION

What is entrapment?

Entrapment occurs when a law enforcement official plants in the mind of an otherwise innocent person the inclination to engage in a criminal act. Merely providing the opportunity to engage in a criminal act does NOT constitute entrapment.

Can a person entrapped into committing a crime be convicted of the crime?

No. Generally, entrapment may serve as an affirmative defense in a criminal prosecution. However, the issue of entrapment is a jury decision. This, of course, means that the defendant is admitting that he or she committed the crime.

B. AVOIDING ENTRAPMENT

How do I know when I am merely providing an opportunity for criminal behavior or entrapping a person into committing a crime?

The basic guideline involves the extent to which you are encouraging, prodding, or enticing the person, and providing him or her with the means to commit the crime.

What are some examples of non-entrapment and entrapment?

Non-entrapment:

1. In an effort to apprehend the perpetrator of some recent car cloutings (breaking and entering) in a parking lot, rangers park a vehicle with camera equipment in plain view on the front seat. They observe the vehicle from the woods and when someone breaks into it, they make an arrest.

2. In an effort to apprehend a rapist who assaulted several women in one of the park areas, a female ranger poses as a sunbather wearing a bikini. When a person tries to assault her, other rangers who have been observing nearby, emerge from their cover and arrest him.

3. To deal with a drug-selling problem, undercover rangers act as dealers and as soon as they make a "deal" with a potential buyer, they arrest him.

4. A ranger receives a call about noise at a particular campsite late at night. She goes to the site and tells the people to quiet down. She leaves the site but sneaks back to see if they have complied. Finding that they are still noisy, she then makes herself known, writes them a citation, and expels them from the campground.

5. A female ranger poses as a prostitute and asks a visitor if he would like to "have a little fun." The visitor asks "How much?" and she gives a price. When he hands her the money the ranger arrests him for solicitation of prostitution.

6. An undercover ranger asks a frequent visitor if he can get him some eagle feathers from an endangered or controlled species. After prompting for several minutes, the visitor finally agrees. When he delivers the feathers, the ranger arrests him.

Entrapment:

1. Rangers hire teenagers to approach the clerk of a park store and persist in asking him to sell them some beer. The clerk, who has no history of selling alcohol to minors, initially refuses, but after they persist for half an hour, he gives in and sells them a six-pack. The rangers then arrest him for selling alcohol to minors.

2. An undercover ranger persists in offering to sell a visitor some marijuana and, after several minutes of persuasion, the visitor finally agrees to buy an ounce, and he is arrested.

3. Posing as visitors, some rangers talk a person into helping them illegally dig for Civil War relics in a park. When the individual digs up the first bullet they cite him for illegal possession of an historical artifact.

4. An undercover ranger asks a frequent visitor if he can get him some eagle feathers from an endangered or controlled species. After prompting for several minutes, the visitor finally agrees. *The ranger provides him with a special trap and tells him where to set it.* When the visitor delivers the feathers, the ranger arrests him.

When contemplating any undercover or "sting" operations, remember that, as a park ranger or other law enforcement officer, your policing role consists primarily of preventing, detecting, and investigating illegal behavior, not testing the moral integrity of the park's visitors. For entrapment issues related to drug enforcement, see Chapter XX.

NOTES

CHAPTER XIII

FIRST AMENDMENT RIGHTS

First Amendment rights include freedom of speech, press, religion, and assembly; they are among the most protected rights of individuals. The Supreme Court has also recognized the right of privacy to be apparent and emanating from the Constitution.

From their onset, parks have been a place for privacy, meditation, political events, demonstrations, sit-ins, meetings, etc. for the purpose of furthering some political, social, personal, or economic cause. Many park systems have viewed this type of park use as counter to the original purpose of the park, and they have attempted to prohibit the activities or remove them from the park property. Occasionally such attempts have led to rioting, mass arrests and injuries.

A. FREEDOM OF SPEECH

1. **Speech**: Freedom of speech is one of the more protected freedoms and generally includes the freedom of expression in most forms. A person has a right to speak in most public locations, though it may be regulated for reasons of real safety under some circumstances. As a note, however, there is no right to be heard. While regulation of park usage will normally accommodate the ranger's needs as well as the visitors', regulations should not be used to exclude unpopular or unpleasant speech.

Obscene language may be dealt with as inappropriate behavior. Language is not obscene, however, merely because it offends particular individuals. The better rule would be to deal with the behavior as being loud or disorderly than merely obscene. As an example, the visitor who merely swears at you in your official capacity is not committing an act that, in and of itself, is necessarily criminal.

2. **Expression**: Expression is normally used to act out some conflict with another group or political position. Such

expression may include burning books, flags, or figures in effigy. This may obviously be restricted to safe areas (not safe from view or notice only) for fires or subject to fire conditions. Other forms of expression may include sit-ins, vigils, pray-ins, or similar protests. These may be controlled so as not to overflow into other special use areas or for real safety concerns. Again, the control should not develop into unnecessary restraint.

3. **Nudity**: Expression has on occasion taken the form of nudity. The use of nudity as expression may be limited to those demonstrations of value, such as a play, and even then it may be limited to a reasonable display. It is possible not to be obscene in the use of nudity. However, nudity, simply for nudity's sake, is not within the protection of the Constitution and may be banned from public areas.

B. FREEDOM OF THE PRESS

Freedom of the press is very similar to speech. Distribution of handbills, papers, etc. may not be halted in public areas as a general rule. Persons do not have to accept the material, however, and individuals littering may be cited or arrested for such activity, but not for the distribution of the material, *per se*.

C. FREEDOM OF RELIGION

Religious services may be conducted within parks so long as they are not dangerous to the participants or others, not unnecessarily intrusive or imposing on others, and within the constraints of park usage. As an example, a religious service may be conducted in the park, even if the religion is not conventional. There is no right to compel others to hear or participate in the activities, however, or to use regularly restricted areas of the park. For example, if an area of the park is closed at midnight, a religious group would not necessarily have a right to enter the closed area for services, without special permission.

D. Official Action

The notion that certain groups are not "using the park for its intended purpose" and, therefore, should be removed and kept from interfering with the "bona fide" visitors is beginning to lose favor with the courts. A balancing of the right of privacy and public use versus compelling state interests seems to be the courts' stance.

As a general rule you, as a park law enforcement official, should not deny non-traditional groups the use of the park if their activities do not truly represent a threat or significant impediment to park operations or visitor freedom.

For example, if a group requests a permit to hold a demonstration against the government's policies toward nuclear arms, such a request should not be denied out of hand because it is not in keeping with the park's "intended purpose." You may, however, be able to restrict some areas and activities of the park for protection of the park. As an example, you may keep the individuals out of areas of habitat restoration or those restricted to hikers when the demonstrators' purpose is to hold a mass meeting, etc. A protest over trail conditions could be controlled by trail access regulation. You could not, however, exclude the group as individuals from entering the trail, provided they meet the appropriate regulations or requirements.

NOTES

CHAPTER XIV

SPECIAL CONSIDERATIONS

A. PURSUIT DRIVING

Although there is no Supreme Court case law that establishes specific guidelines governing law enforcement officers' use of pursuit and response driving, traditional civil litigation in this area has evolved which suggests that the indiscriminate use of pursuit driving may result in an officer's being held liable for any injuries or property damage that results. Because a large proportion of all high speed pursuits engaged in by officers results in injury, the probability of civil litigation is high.

Every park law enforcement agency should have a vehicle pursuit policy that restricts vehicle pursuits in terms of such variables as: maximum allowable speed, maximum duration, regulations regarding adherence to traffic control signs and signals, type of suspect/offense for which high-speed pursuits are allowed, etc. This policy should be made known to every ranger, with the warning that it should be adhered to or the ranger will risk the loss of his or her qualified good faith immunity defense, should an incident ever occur that precipitates civil litigation. Similarly, guidelines should be promulgated regarding limitations on other types of response driving (e.g., to an accident, fire, call for assistance, etc.).

B. DEALING WITH JUVENILES

1. **Juvenile status:** Juveniles, normally persons under the age of eighteen, may be treated differently from adults. Juveniles are always presumed to be in the custody of someone, their parents, a guardian, a person *in loco parentis* (acting in the place of a parent) or some similar relationship.

2. **Custody:** Juveniles in need of supervision for their protection may be taken into custody when there is suspicion

or evidence indicating that the child needs care (is dependent and neglected), or is abused.

A juvenile may also be taken into custody if there is suspicion or evidence that he or she is, is about to be, or has been involved in a delinquent act (behavior that would be criminal if committed by an adult) or unruly behavior (acts peculiar to juveniles such as: run-away, truancy, drinking, smoking, out after curfew, etc., depending on the law of the respective jurisdiction).

3. **Officer's options**: Juveniles committing acts that cause park law enforcement officers to intervene may be dealt with in many ways, but as a rule it should be in "the best interest of the juvenile." Obviously, as a park officer, you have more authority to inquire into a youth's age, to inquire into suspicious activity where a juvenile is involved, and to question a juvenile to determine the presence of appropriate adult supervision. You may also counsel or caution the youth or take him or her into custody for any of the appropriate reasons. Of course, you may still act to protect the public as well as the juvenile.

What if I take a juvenile into custody?

If you take a juvenile into custody, you may still be civilly liable for false arrest; however, it is easier to support a need for a juvenile's custody than when dealing with an adult. Paramount in the process is the segregating of youthful offenders from general offender populations and getting them to an appropriate judicial hearing as soon as possible. They must be protected and taken to appropriate authorities quickly.

4. **Constitutional protections**: While juveniles are subject to more restrictions and open to more scrutiny, they are accorded most of the same basic constitutional protections as adults (e.g., an exception would be the right to a jury trial and transcript). This simply means that the need for protection and action in the best interest of the juvenile has been added. A juvenile may be taken into custody (i.e., arrested) in the same manner as an adult. The age of the offender will dictate the force and physical restraints that are

allowed. A juvenile may be questioned about activities, but the Miranda warnings should always be used where the juvenile is suspected of delinquent (criminal if adult) behavior. As a ranger, you must be sensitive to the needs, fear, confusion, and youthful condition of the juvenile and you should normally assume that the juvenile cannot waive constitutional rights without counsel or the parents or guardians being present.

Probable cause is very important when dealing with juvenile offenders. Mere suspicion is not adequate to support the taking of a juvenile into custody for delinquent or unruly behavior, but may be adequate for an investigative stop even when it would not be for an adult. *Terry* does not specifically identify what is required to make a stop of an adult, and the standard is even less stringent for juveniles because of the requirement to act in their best interest. As a rule of thumb, the adult could leave the mere suspicion scene; however, a juvenile could not. A good rule for you as a park officer is to act in the best interest of the juvenile and in good faith, and you will normally be correct.

Juveniles facing a disciplinary hearing will be accorded the same court procedures and standards of evidence for proof; however, juveniles are not constitutionally entitled to a jury trial in a delinquency hearing. Ordinarily, juveniles at a more advanced age (e.g., over the age of fourteen or sixteen) and charged with more serious delinquent behavior (serious crimes such as murder, rape, armed robbery, or kidnapping) or repeat offenders may be given a waiver hearing by the juvenile court so that they can be tried as an adult.

5. Contributing to the delinquency of a minor:
If an adult is contributing to the delinquency of a minor, he or she may be arrested on that ground. You should be aware of the appropriate laws of your jurisdiction on this subject. As an example, an adult selling alcohol to a juvenile contrary to the law could be arrested or cited for contributing to the delinquency of a minor in most jurisdictions. Also, an adult accompanying a group of disorderly juveniles in the park could be cited or arrested if the adult persists in his or her behavior or refuses to make the group conform to appropri-

ate conduct. The juveniles could, of course, be taken into custody for their conduct.

Likewise, in most jurisdictions an adult who is engaging in sexual activity with a (non-spouse) juvenile, is contributing to the juvenile's delinquency.

6. Stopping juveniles:

When I stop a vehicle containing several youths and ask them to empty their pockets and they flee, may I take them into custody?

Yes. The flight under those circumstances is adequate probable cause to take them into custody.

If I approach a group of young people on a blanket in the park and ask if they are having fun and they run, is that adequate probable cause?

No, not without other factors or observations. It would, however, justify a stop and, if warranted, a frisk.

May I ask juveniles found in a public bathroom in the park what they are doing?

Yes, particularly if there are any supporting circumstances such as smoke, beer cans, liquor bottles, a noisy crowd, etc.

If I see several youthful visitors drinking beer may I ask for their identifications?

Yes. You may ask for the identification and follow up with more inquiry of those without proper identification or those under the drinking age. The people should be able to prove that they are adults, unless it is apparent.

May I detain a youthful suspect?

You may detain a youthful suspect more easily than an adult if you have the requisite reasonable suspicion, but you must act more quickly to secure a detention hearing and keep the youth segregated from adults during the detention.

May I stop youthful boaters and water skiers for reckless conduct?

Yes, you may stop them as you could adults. You may stop them more easily if adult supervision is lacking because their conduct is dangerous to them and to others, and you are acting in their best interest.

C. DEALING WITH MILITARY PERSONNEL

1. Members of the American Armed Forces

Rangers, fish and wildlife officers and other land management personnel are often faced with having to take law enforcement action against someone who is a member of the American Armed Forces. It is important to know that these situations often necessitate special procedures. It is possible that you would not know that a person was in the military, in which instance you should proceed as you would in any other situation. If it becomes apparent to you that a person is in the military, you should proceed as noted below.

May I write a member of the Armed Services a citation?

Yes, if you encounter a person engaging in an act for which you would normally write a citation, even if he or she is on active duty with some branch of the Armed Services, you may write the citation.

May I give a member of the Armed Services a summons to court to answer for violating a law or regulation which I have authority to enforce?

Yes, if you would normally give a summons to an individual for committing the offense, you may give the summons to the member of the Armed Services.

May I arrest a member of the Armed Services?

Yes. As an example, you work in an area near an Army base, and you apprehend an off-duty soldier for driving while intoxicated. He tells you that he has to be back to the base in half an hour. You may arrest the individual as you would anyone else.

Once I arrest a member of the Armed Services, is the judicial process any different from what it would be for anyone else?

No. The judicial process for arrest, detention, providing constitutional rights, or care is no different in so far as your actions are concerned. There may, however, be a different process for the military person in the system. If the matter is merely a citation and it is resolved, the matter should be considered closed. If, however, circumstances, either because of impact or seriousness, warrant further action the nearest appropriate prosecutor's office and the nearest military installation (military police or shore patrol) should be notified, giving the charges, name, rank, serial number, military organization, if known, and installation.

2. Members of foreign armed forces

Are members of foreign armed forces treated any differently from members of the American Armed Forces?

No. You should, however, notify the United States Attorney's Office or the United States State Department of the arrest, including the charges, name, rank and serial number. For example, a foreign navy vessel is moored in a harbor nearby, and you apprehend several sailors on shore leave selling cocaine in your park. They should be arrested and the procedures followed as previously noted.

D. ESTABLISHING PROBABLE CAUSE WITH INTOXICATED DRIVERS

With respect to visitor safety, one of the most important enforcement functions you serve is to detect and apprehend people who are driving under the influence of drugs or alcohol. In order to arrest a person for driving under the influence (D.U.I.) and have the person's blood or breath analyzed for the presence of alcohol, you must first establish probable cause that the person is, indeed, D.U.I. In some jurisdictions this is still a relatively easy matter, but because the nation's laws against drunk driving are becoming more punitive, there is also an increasing sophistication among defense attorneys that enables them to more competently discredit you or your testimony when a D.U.I. case reaches trial. In order to present a good case against a drunk driver, it is necessary that you be systematic and thorough in your development of probable cause and in the documentation of your case. Although each court may be different, there are some general guidelines which, if followed, will make it much more difficult for a defense attorney to win a D.U.I case for his or her client. The following guidelines are presented to help you develop probable cause in a D.U.I. case and then not lose the case when you go to court.

Before you can have a blood or breath test administered to a suspected D.U.I., you must have probable cause that he or she is D.U.I. and effect an arrest based upon your probable cause. You establish your probable cause by observing (1) the violator's driving behavior, (2) other driver behaviors during your traffic stop, and (3) the driver's performance on selected field sobriety tests.

What are some kinds of initial observations of driver behavior that may be used to raise my suspicions that someone is driving under the influence?

1. weaving or crossing the center line several times
2. straddling the center line
3. driving considerably below the speed limit
4. failing to dim headlights to oncoming traffic
5. speeding
6. ignoring traffic signals or signs
7. littering
8. excessive use of brakes
9. turning with a wide radius
10. following too closely
11. almost striking another vehicle or object
12. driving off designated roadways

*During my stop of a potential D.U.I. offender,
what types of observations might increase my
suspicions?*

1. delayed stopping response to your emergency lights or
   siren
2. excessive movement of occupants in vehicle
3. partial roll-down of driver's window
4. red, watery, or glassy eyes
5. flushed face
6. slow or slurred speech
7. odor of intoxicating beverage (alcohol itself does not
   have an odor)
8. fumbling in wallet for operator's license
9. presence of alcoholic beverages in vehicle
10. delays in responding to requests (e.g., to turn down
    volume on radio, to provide operator's license or vehi-
    cle registration, etc.)
11. excessive belligerence
12. driver sick/vomiting

*If I suspect that a driver may be under the influ-
ence and I attempt to remove him or her from the
vehicle, what else should I look for?*

1. awkward or unsteady gait
2. attempts to lean on vehicle for support
3. difficulty maintaining balance while exiting vehicle
4. difficulty maintaining balance while standing
5. indications of stomach sickness, vomiting, etc.

*If I continue to suspect D.U.I. and want to admin-
ister field sobriety tests, what points are relevant
to developing probable cause for an arrest?*

1. Before using any field sobriety tests, you should (a) be
   trained in their administration by an expert, and (b) have
   an opportunity to practice executing them and administering them. Remember, you will probably be asked to
   demonstrate these tests in court.

2. Demonstrate each test you plan to administer just prior
   to administering it.

106

3. Administer more than one test (at least three would be preferable).

4. If driver fails any test, give him or her at least two more chances to perform it.

5. Record the order of tests given.

6. Record the number of attempts that driver made to pass each test.

7. Record the specific way in which driver failed each test.

8. Remember to make note of any statements the driver may make about speech impediments, inner ear infections, medication, or other conditions that may affect his or her balance or test performance.

What are some of the generally accepted field sobriety tests?

Several different types of tests have been developed and, before deciding on the ones you will use, it is a good idea to find out which ones are preferred by the prosecutor(s) and judge(s) who may be dealing with your D.U.I. cases. Below is a list of some of the more commonly accepted field sobriety tests:

1. Tests of balance:
   a. one leg stand test: driver stands on one leg, holds other leg straight out in front, about six inches off the ground for 30 seconds (driver counts slowly to 30 while looking at the raised foot).
   b. heel-to-toe test: driver walks a real or imaginary straight line heel-to-toe for nine steps, pivots slowly on the left foot, and walks back nine steps; Driver counts the steps out loud and watches his or her feet while walking.
   c. heel-to-toe/pick-up-coin test: driver walks heel-to-toe for about nine steps, bends over to pick up a coin from the ground, and then stands up straight.

2. Tests of coordination:
   a. finger-to-nose test: driver shuts eyes, tips head back, extends arms out to side and then attempts to touch nose by first placing the index finger of one hand then the index finger of the other, on nose.

3. Tests involving speech:
   a. recite the complete alphabet, preferably by beginning with some letter in the middle such as "G".
   b. counting-fingers test: Using one hand only, driver counts fingers while simultaneously touching thumb to the four fingers, beginning with the little finger, going to the index, and then counts backwards beginning with the index and going to the little finger. Thus, the counting sequence is "one, two, three, four, four, three, two, one," and the appropriate fingers must be touched. When driver finishes with one hand, he or she then counts fingers on other hand in same manner.

4. Horizontal gaze nystagmus test: This test is based on the fact that alcohol impairment usually affects the eyes' ability to efficiently follow objects moving back and forth in a horizontal plane. The driver is asked to hold his or her head still while visually following a moving object (e.g., a pen) as the officer moves it back and forth in front of the driver's face.

What information should be included in the incident report that I will take to court?

In addition to the standard information, you should include the following:

1. your initial observations that led you to make the traffic stop

2. any significant observations about how the violator responded to your request to "pull over"

3. any relevant observations about the violator's physical and verbal behavior, odors, liquor in the vehicle, etc. when you first made your contact

4. any relevant observations about how violator acted or what violator said when he or she exited the vehicle

5. what field sobriety tests you administered, the order in which they were given, how many times each was attempted, whether they were passed or failed and, if they were failed, in what specific ways they were failed

6. any other observations about the violator's behavior that may be relevant, e.g., general demeanor, vomit, belligerence, statements about drinking, etc.

What if a suspected D.U.I. refuses to take a field sobriety, a blood or breath test?

Most states have "implied consent" laws which means that a refusal to take the test results in loss of driving privileges for a certain period of time. However, it is important to remember that you may be able to successfully prosecute a D.U.I. case based upon your general observations of the driver's behavior before and during the traffic stop as well as on other evidence that may be available (e.g., open liquor bottles). In other words, in the case of uncooperative drivers, the results of field sobriety tests or blood or breath samples are not necessarily required for conviction. Clearly, in such cases, as well as all D.U.I. cases, the quality of your observations and report will be critical.

E. MODEL INVENTORY POLICY

It shall be the policy of _____ Park to inventory all private or abandoned property that is impounded, regardless of reason. This policy is to be followed in its entirety by all personnel. The purpose of the inventory procedure is to protect any valuable property that may be part of an impoundment and protect the park from the possibility of negligence in the loss of private property. The inventory procedure is **NOT** to be used as an alternative to obtaining a search warrant in those cases in which it is suspected that evidence of criminal activity may be present with the impounded property.

Inventorying impounded vehicles: When any vehicle is impounded by park personnel, it will be completely inventoried and will include the passenger compartment, the glove box, the trunk, the spare tire well, ashtrays, and any unlocked or unsealed containers, regardless of size. Examples of containers would include, but are not limited to, such things as: backpacks, handbags, purses, film canisters, flashlights, wallets, picnic baskets, athletic bags, camera cases, glasses cases, diaper bags, luggage of all types, tool boxes and kits, first aid kits, plastic or paper bags, tackle boxes, shoes, boots, rifle and pistol cases, cardboard boxes, etc. Any containers that are locked or sealed (e.g., with strapping tape) will be inventoried as single units, without opening them. Wheel covers and hubcaps will be removed and placed in the trunk to secure them. The engine area will be checked for anything of special value (e.g., chrome parts).

When the inventory is complete, all items of value will be secured, and a written record of everything of value will be made and signed by the inventorying officer(s).

Inventorying non-vehicles: In the event that other property is impounded (e.g., boats, camping equipment, camera equipment, backpacks, handbags, etc.), a complete inventory will be made and will include inventorying all unlocked or unsealed containers. Each locked or sealed container will be inventoried as a single unit without opening it.

When the inventory is complete, all items of value will be secured, and a written record of everything of value will be made and signed by the inventorying officer(s). All property found and in custody of the Park that was not obtained pursuant to a seizure will be inventoried.

Evidence: If, during the inventory procedure, evidence or fruits or instrumentalities of a crime should be inadvertently discovered, the inventorying officer(s) shall stop the inventory immediately, secure the property being inventoried, maintain the chain of custody of the found evidence, and notify supervisory personnel. The purpose for this procedure is to allow a decision to be made as to whether to seek a warrant to search the impounded vehicle or property.

F. Diplomatic Immunity

Persons whom you have detained for committing violations of park regulations or committing crimes on park property and who claim diplomatic immunity may be held to verify their diplomatic status. In such cases it is your responsibility to immediately contact the U.S. State Department to verify their claim. Follow the instructions of the appropriate State Department authority. During this time treat the individual(s) with respect and care and do not conduct a search of their persons or property. You may, of course, frisk to protect yourself or others, if warranted. You should also notify the United States or State's Attorney of the person's identity and the offense. If the matter is minor, you should consult your supervisor. The person with diplomatic immunity may be merely cited or expelled from the park and the same authorities notified.

NOTES

CHAPTER XV

AN OVERVIEW OF LIABILITY

Concern over liability issues has been the driving force behind major changes in law enforcement procedures, selection standards, training, deployment, supervision and retention. In fact, it is fair to say that it has been the primary driving force behind law enforcement reform in general. In spite of its importance, however, many in park law enforcement are relatively unaware of the nature of liability and liability exposure and how these concepts impact the law enforcement function in park settings. What follows is a review of these concepts and the categories of liability.

What is legal liability?

Legal liability is the responsibility under law a person has for his or her actions or inactions.

What is legal duty?

Legal duty can be defined as that which a person is legally obligated to do or refrain from doing. Generally a person has a duty to exercise reasonable care to avoid subjecting other persons or their property to unreasonable risks of harm.

Legal duty may also be that which one should do, based on the probability or foreseeability of injury to a party. As public servants, park rangers have imposed on them a duty that they must meet for ethical and professional reasons. Carrying out this legal duty will also reduce their exposure to liability.

What is the "public duty doctrine"?

It refers to a duty owed by a law enforcement officer to the public, as a whole, to provide for the general safety and welfare; it is not owed to any particular individual as such. As an example, rangers have a general duty to remove drunk drivers from park roads.

What is a "special duty" owed to an individual?

It is a duty owed to a particular individual or class of individuals that results from a special relationship. For example, there is a special duty incumbent on a ranger to remove a person incapacitated in the middle of a roadway to a place of safety. The special duty is imposed on the ranger because of the office and the resultant training and skills to provide for safety for those unable to secure their own.

In a civil lawsuit what options for obtaining relief are open to the plaintiff?

a. *Injunction*: the plaintiff may sue to have the defendant cease an action.

b. *Commence action*: the plaintiff may also sue to have the defendant begin an action (e.g., put up a fence).

c. *Damages*: the plaintiff may sue to obtain a monetary judgment from the defendant to "balance the wrong" of some act. Direct damages cover direct losses as a result of the negligent act and compensation for such things as pain and suffering. Punitive damages are sometimes awarded in addition to direct damages as a "fine" the defendant has to pay to the plaintiff as a result of some grossly negligent, willful, or reckless act that inflicted the loss or injury.

***What are the various categories of liability, and
how are they defined?***

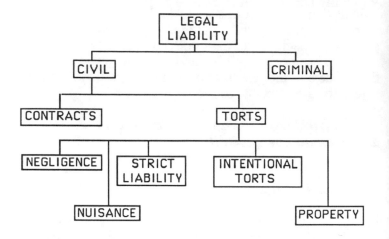

Legal liability may be divided into two main categories:
criminal and *civil*.

Criminal Liability: Criminal liability is the culpability or
responsibility for an act or failure to act that has been defined
by law as a harm against the state. The violation of criminal
laws amounts to an act against the state (as well as the person who was the actual victim of the act). In other words, in
criminal liability, it is the state (public as a whole) which has
been wronged.

Civil Liability: Civil liability is the culpability or responsibility for an act or failure to act that caused a loss or harm
to another individual, but is not considered to be a wrong
against the state.

What are the categories of civil liability?

There are two principal types of civil liability:

1. liability involving **contracts.**
2. liability involving **torts.** This category would be of
    most interest to those in park law enforcement.

What is a tort?

A **tort** may be thought of as loss or harm sustained by a person that provides the legal basis for a lawsuit.

Are there different types of torts?

Yes. Torts may be divided into the following types:
1. Negligence
2. Strict liability
3. Intentional torts
4. Nuisance torts
5. Property torts

What is "liability" in tort law?

Liability in tort law is a creation of individual case decisions, commonly referred to as the common law. Generally, conduct may be tortious only if there is a legal duty to act or avoid an act, which results in injury. No jurisdiction has attempted to completely codify this area of law. Accordingly, when we talk about tort law we do so without definition; however, we are seeking principles and rules to avoid liability.

Perhaps the easiest way to understand this law is to recognize that it is a part of civil law, i.e., it is concerned with what the individual can do to find remedy for an injury sustained from the action or inaction of another party. Remember, however, that a civil wrong may also be a criminal wrong and, therefore, punishable by the state.

What is the purpose of tort law?

There are three purposes in this area of law:
1. Compensate the victim: in so far as possible to "make whole" the victim, as much as the money paid in damages can.
2. Provide justice: by requiring those responsible to pay the determined damages.
3. Deter others: society is made safer by deterring dangerous behavior which creates injury.

What is required to demonstrate tort liability?

Liability requires the following four elements:
1. A **duty** owed to the injured party by the party responsible for the injury.
2. A **breach** of that duty because of the action or inaction of the party responsible for the injury.
3. An **injury** to the party to whom the duty was owed.
4. A **causal connection** between 2 and 3 above.

What is meant by "proximate cause"?

Proximate cause is a legal fiction used to limit a defendant's liability. It requires that the injury has a reasonable relationship to the tortious conduct. As a rule, one must consider whether the consequences of the act were foreseeable and whether or not intervening causes exist. Normally, liability is limited to individuals who were in the foreseeable area of hazard and where the foreseeability was present when the injury took place.

A defendant, therefore, may be liable if he or she could have foreseen any harm from his or her actions or lack thereof. Furthermore, the defendant may be liable even if it was not foreseeable, unless the court finds that the likelihood that the conduct would cause the resultant harm was too remote or unusual.

NOTES

CHAPTER XVI

TORT LIABILITY: NEGLIGENCE

What are the different types of torts?

The categories of torts include negligence, nuisance, strict liability, intentional torts and property.

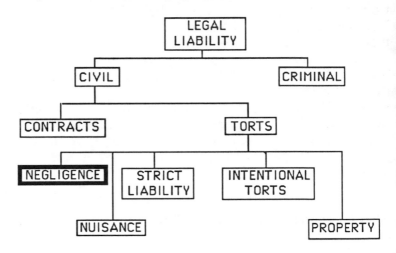

What is Negligence?

Negligence is an act or failure to act that results in loss or injury to an innocent party. Negligence is conduct (whether intentional or not) that fails to conform to legal standards. A jury makes a determination of negligence by asking whether a defendant's conduct was the same as the fictional "reasonably prudent person," if placed in the same circumstances.

Must I be perfect?

The law requires no one to be perfect but only that he or she act as the reasonably prudent person would in a similar situation. The reasonably prudent person is generally one with normal or average attributes. However, in cases in which people must possess more knowledge or higher qualifications, skills, or intellect than the average reasonably prudent person, they may be held to the higher level. Park rangers would fall into such a category, and they must exhibit the appropriate standard of care.

What is meant by "standard of care?"

Standard of care (in negligence cases) represents the level of care a reasonable person of similar skills and qualifications would use under similar circumstances. It is the criterion by which courts evaluate behavior; the fictional "reasonable person." The resultant standard of care is normally couched in terms of "ordinary care," "due care," or "reasonable care." Implicit in this legal doctrine is the notion that the standard of reasonableness is not normally met if a person engages in an act or failure to act that results in an injury or loss to someone else. Furthermore, reasonableness implies that if the person either *knew or should have known* that his or her behavior could be the proximate cause of injury to another, then an acceptable standard of care is not normally met.

Thus, a defendant's liability for an injury is founded upon what he or she knew or should have known of a risk, and that a sufficient degree of probability is present that will cause a harm to a plaintiff. A park ranger must understand the parameters of reasonableness as applicable to his or her duties under the law. No provision is made for any weaknesses of an officer, so any forgetful, careless, ignorant, foolish, rash, impetuous, timid, or clumsy person is held to the "reasonable person" standard whether he or she can conform or not.

How are standards of care established?

Standards of care are often created by case law, guidelines for juries, legislative histories, legislation, and rules of law, but are generally left to juries. Generally, the violation of a law (statute) is negligence *per se*, which means that if the defendant fails to introduce evidence which excuses the violation, the negligence as to the defendant is conclusively established.

Give some examples of reasonably prudent conduct and adequate standard of care.

1. A ranger would be held to a requirement of competency with firearms or first aid techniques. The knowledge of the use of firearms in parks, under all weather conditions and times of the day, would be the assumed reasonably prudent level. The ranger would be assumed to know more about first aid procedures than the average lay person; however, a doctor would be presumed to conform to an even higher standard. Furthermore, once you assume the role and begin carrying out a duty, you must follow through with the appropriate standard of care. Failure to do so may result in a finding of negligence.

2. Generally, rangers would be expected to have increased capacity to anticipate emergencies and respond to them. As an example, in a very heavy rain storm, rangers should automatically remove people from potential flood areas or respond adequately if caught by a surprise flood. The fact that a flood has not occurred before is not a defense; the question is how the reasonably prudent person with a ranger's skills would respond.

3. One is supposed to reasonably anticipate or foresee some types of conduct of others. The ranger, in particular, is supposed to foresee circumstances in which he or she can expect negligent or criminal conduct by others or in which the ranger may instigate behavior in a person that would subject others to the risk or harm.

What are the different degrees of negligence?

The popular degrees of negligence are **slight, ordinary,** and **gross.**

Slight negligence is a failure to exercise great or unusual care.

Ordinary negligence is the failure to meet the mythical "reasonable person" standard of care.

122

Gross negligence is a failure to exercise slight care.

Some conduct is more dangerous than others and requires a special duty. Those responsible for dangerous instrumentalities must exercise a higher degree of care or reasonableness under the particular circumstances. A ranger operating a shooting range would fall in this category.

What is reckless conduct?

Reckless conduct (sometimes referred to as willful and wanton misconduct) occurs when a person knew or should have known that his or her conduct creates an unreasonable risk of harm and the risk, in degree or probability, is relatively high that harm will occur. In reckless conduct a defendant must be conscious that the conduct creates a relatively high risk of harm, as opposed to negligent conduct in which no awareness of risk is required. However, reckless conduct lacks the certainty of outcome found in intentional torts.

With respect to negligence, what is required to demonstrate the existence of liability?

The plaintiff carries the burden of proof and must demonstrate, with a preponderance of the evidence, the following:

1. There was a legal duty to perform, with respect to another person, in a certain way or to certain standards.

2. There was a breach of that legal duty to perform.

3. There was some loss or injury sustained by the victim of the negligent act or failure to act.

4. The negligent performance was the proximate cause (i.e., in the direct causal chain) of the loss or injury.

Again, what is proximate cause?

Proximate cause is something which, in natural unbroken sequence, produces a result and without which the injury could not have occurred. It is the cause of an accident or injury. It is, however, not necessarily the closest thing in time or space to the injury and not necessarily the event that set things in motion. The notion of proximate cause is very important because, for liability to be established, it is a requirement that the defendant's actions be a proximate cause of the loss or injuries.

What is "res ipsa loquitur"?

Res ipsa loquitur: The "thing speaks for itself" rule is one of circumstantial evidence. If a plaintiff can show that his or her injury was (1) caused by an instrumentality or condition which was under the exclusive control or management of the defendant, (2) under circumstances in which the plaintiff's injury would not have occurred unless the defendant was negligent, and (3) that the plaintiff did not cause the injury-causing incident, then the jury may assume, without further proof, that the defendant's conduct was negligent and therefore the cause of injury. As an example, when a plaintiff is able to demonstrate that he or she was placed unconscious in a ranger patrol car behind the screen with the doors closed, and should not have sustained a broken arm, but did, the jury may assume that the ranger was negligent and therefore liable, unless the ranger is able to prove something else was the cause.

What are some of the variables affecting negligence liability?

1. *Contributory negligence*: Contributory negligence asserts that a plaintiff's conduct was such that it created an unreasonable risk of harm to the plaintiff when combined with the defendant's negligence. In most jurisdictions, contributory negligence mitigates rather than negates liability. Normally, contributory negligence is not a defense if the defendant's conduct falls in the reckless conduct and strict liability categories.

2. *Comparative negligence*: Comparative negligence generally allows a distribution of liability and, therefore, of damages, between the plaintiff and defendant.

3. *Last clear chance*: When a plaintiff (or his or her property) is in a danger from which he or she cannot extricate him- or herself, and the defendant has an opportunity to prevent the harm, the defendant is not permitted to use the plaintiff's prior negligence as a defense to negate his or her own negligence.

4. *Assumption of risk*: In most jurisdictions, if a plaintiff voluntarily assumes the risk of harm that arises from a defendant's reckless or negligent conduct, he or she may not recover for the particular harm. The risk must be assumable and the potential harm apparent. There appears to be a trend toward restricting this defense.

What is vicarious liability?

In negligence cases, **vicarious liability** allows a person (and a legal entity) to be liable for another's behavior when a relationship to supervise, aid, or train exists, and the supervisor either knew or should have known that the conduct of the subordinate would be likely to result in harm to another. As an example, if a supervisory ranger was aware that a ranger under his or her authority tended to be abusive, and the ranger was brutal in the handling of an arrestee, the supervisor and entity could be found liable for the injury. The ability to remedy the matter is in the hands of the supervisor; therefore, the liability is imputed to the ranger and the entity.

In some jurisdictions employers are liable for all conduct of their employees while acting within the scope of employment, whether or not the employer knew or should have known of the likelihood of the harm.

The park and supervisors most often will be placed in a position of liability for the acts of rangers if the rangers are acting within the color of law. The scope of employment factor is a question for the jury and they may take into consideration any factors having a bearing on the employment relationship.

NOTES

CHAPTER XVII

TORT LIABILITY:
STRICT LIABILITY, INTENTIONAL
TORTS, AND NUISANCE

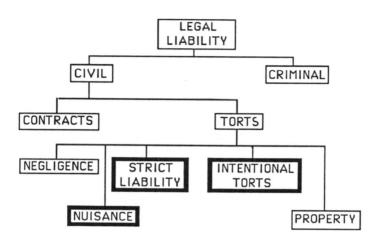

A. Strict liability

What is strict liability?

Strict liability refers to situations in which a person may be held liable even though the person exhibited reasonable care and did nothing "wrong." Having to "make good" on a product that turned out to be defective would be an example of strict liability.

While strict liability may be imposed in other areas, in a park setting it is routinely associated with abnormally dangerous activity. Factors that may be associated with the rule are:

1. What is the extent of risk? That is, how high a degree of risk of harm exists, and what is the likelihood that the harm to others will be great?

2. Is there an ability to eliminate the risk? If the risk remains after reasonable care is taken to avoid it, the possibility of strict liability may still exist.

3. Is it an abnormal activity? The further away from common usage, the greater the exposure to strict liability.

4. Location: Is the activity being conducted in an improper place?

5. Societal interests: Does the activity's value exceed its social value?

What are some limitations on strict liability?

1. Proximate cause requires the harm to result from the abnormal danger for liability to be established.

2. Legislative action may preclude strict liability, or legislation authorizing one to carry on the activity will normally exclude strict liability. Legislation may also create strict liability in certain situations.

B. Intentional tort

What is an intentional tort?

An **intentional tort** occurs when the loss or harm caused by the action or inaction was intended by the person inflicting the tort.

What is intent?

Intent is a desire to cause a particular consequence by a specific act or the belief that the end result is a substantial certainty of the act.

Examples of Intentional Torts

What is a battery?

Battery is offensive physical contact with another or with something in his or her immediate control or possession. Something as simple as turning another's horse or knocking off a hat could be a battery.

What is assault?

If a person intentionally places another in apprehension of an imminent battery, an **assault** has occurred. There must be an intent to cause the contact; the plaintiff must be aware (apprehension) of the act before its termination; and there must be an apparent intent and ability to carry out the threat at that time.

As an example, a visitor firing a weapon at another, but missing, does not commit an assault unless the person at whom the shot was directed is aware of the incident and, therefore, apprehensive of the shot. This is distinguished from criminal assault, which does not require knowledge or apprehension on the part of the intended victim, because the action is viewed as being against the public as a whole (sovereign). Furthermore, assault requires that no privilege to use force exists. For example, a ranger physically expelling a rowdy party from a campground would not generally be liable for an assault.

What is false imprisonment?

The intentional confinement of a person by an individual, absent legal authority, is **false imprisonment**, absent specific legal authority. As an example, the detention by a ranger of an individual for shoplifting in the park shop could be false imprisonment, absent probable cause for arrest or statutory relief permitting a brief detention for investigation.

What is intentional or reckless infliction of emotional distress?

A defendant is subject to liability to a plaintiff for **emotional distress**, or resulting harm, that is caused by extreme and outrageous behavior he or she intentionally performed. Abuse of power by a law enforcement officer which exceeds the ordinary means of persuasion or demand is designated as a flagrant abuse of power in the nature of extortion and, as such, may be actionable.

What are the defenses to liability for intentional torts?

1. *Privilege*: As a rule privilege is found by consent or an act of law, irrespective of consent. For example, a ranger is privileged to use reasonable force to apprehend an individual.

2. *Consent*: When one is willing for the conduct to occur, there is consent which is almost always a defense to any tort. For example, a person consents to battery in a football game, but this does not extend to excessive force which would exceed the consent.

3. *Self defense and defense of others*: A person is normally privileged to use reasonable force as is necessary to protect him- or herself from immediate physical harm threatened by the intentional or negligent conduct of another person. This includes the use of self defense against an assault, false imprisonment, or a negligently caused harm. Excessive force is not permitted, and any force used after the person extending the original conduct is subdued, disarmed, helpless, or has withdrawn from the fracas is not permitted.

    Likewise, force may be utilized to come to the defense of another under the same circumstances that the third party would be privileged to defend him- or herself against. However, if the intervening defender is wrong, that mistake, no matter how reasonable, is irrelevant, and the defender may be liable for assault, battery, etc.

A person with a duty to protect another person or his or her property is privileged, under law, to use reasonable force or confinement, appropriate to the occasion, to effect the duty.

d. *Defending and recovering property*: One in possession of property may utilize reasonable force to expel another from or prevent trespass on property or prevent the taking of personal property. This is true even though the force used would normally be an assault, battery, or false imprisonment. Only necessary force is permitted, and any force likely to cause death or great bodily harm is not permitted.

Also, concealed traps, spring guns, and vicious animals operate at the risk of the party putting them in place.

One may use limited self-help to recapture one's property wrongfully and forcibly taken from one's possession, even where there is a claim of right, or if obtained by fraud or duress. The effort to recapture the property must begin immediately upon the dispossession or after learning of it so that it is a continuous, uninterrupted act. Demand to return the property must be made first. Then, if the demand is futile, only reasonable force, not force likely to cause serious bodily harm, may be used. Mistake as to the need for the force is no defense to liability.

e. *Necessity*: The defense of necessity may be utilized when defending one's person or property from some harm in a manner that results in harm to the plaintiff. Public necessity will be the defense which a ranger would most often use. For example, a ranger sets a back fire to stop an encroaching fire and the fire burns another's house; it would almost always be entirely excused so long as the reasonable care standard is met. The danger affects the park or the community so that public interest is involved and, therefore, the privilege is allowed.

f. *Authority of law*: Individuals acting under the authority of law are privileged, under appropriate circumstances, to commit acts that would normally be assault, battery, imprisonment, and trespass. A park law enforcement officer could, therefore, physically restrain (battery) an individual, handcuff him or her (confinement), and transport the person to the station, if it is in furtherance of reasonable law enforcement.

Ministerial v. discretionary acts: A ranger, using appropriate discretion, may in good faith determine how to act (e.g., whether to arrest or close an area of the park) and is privileged to do so . Ministerial (obligatory) acts, on the other hand, are not in the privileged category, regardless of good faith, if done improperly.

C. Nuisance

In liability, what is an action for nuisance?

Nuisance refers to conduct, and generally is identified as either *public* or *private*. Private nuisance, a particular activity or thing which unreasonably and substantially interferes with a person's enjoyment of property, is normally of little consideration in the park setting. Public nuisance, on the other hand, is an unreasonable interference with a common collective right. Generally, this includes interference with public peace and safety, health and comfort, and public morals. These rights must be common to the public.

NOTES

CHAPTER XVIII

TORT LIABILITY:
OTHER LIABILITY CONSIDERATIONS

A. Liability Considerations for Employers and Employees

Does the employer-employee relationship generate any special concerns?

The employer-employee relationship creates liability for and toward one another.

1. *Vicarious Liability*: An employer may be vicariously liable for the acts of his or her employee if the employee was acting within the scope of his or her employment. As noted previously, the park and supervisors most often will be placed in a position of liability for the acts of rangers if the rangers are acting within the color of law. The scope of employment factor is a question for the jury and they may take into consideration any factors having a bearing on the employment relationship.

2. *Intentional torts*: If an employee is acting within the scope of his or her employment, and intentionally commits a tortious act in furtherance of the employment, the employer is vicariously liable. Where there is a special duty of protection between an employer and a plaintiff, the employer may be vicariously liable for an injury in breach of that duty, whether committed in furtherance of the employer's interest or for personal reasons. For example, if there is a medical emergency call from the campground and the ranger does not respond, the employer inherits the responsibility.

3. *Direct liability*: The employer may be directly liable, not vicariously liable, for the conduct of the employee. Most often the employer may be directly liable for such acts on his or her part in selecting, hiring, training, in-

structing, testing, supervising, evaluating, retraining, reassignment, etc. The employer may also be directly liable for the consequences of commanding or authorizing an employee's act.

In general, to escape liability, employers must provide a safe place to work with safe equipment or tools adequate for the job, with adequate competent fellow employees, under adequate supervision, and with training necessary to accomplish the work.

B. Liability and Contractors

How does the use of independent contractors affect liability exposure?

As a rule, an employer is not vicariously liable for physical harm caused by an independent contractor or its employees. However, there are exceptions to this rule, which include such things as: negligent standards and contract minimums, selection, instruction, failure to inspect and monitor work, retention of control and supervision, and duties of special relationships.

C. Liability Involving Interference with Federal Constitutional Rights

Persons interfering with another's constitutional rights under color of law may be sued under 42 U.S.C.A. § 1983. (See Chapter II section on Civil Liability).

D. Misrepresentation and Defamation

What is negligent misrepresentation?

An erroneous misrepresentation about another, even if honestly believed to be true, is actionable if it fails to meet professional or business standards, and there is a failure to exercise reasonable care in determining the truth.

What is defamation?

Generally, a false statement about another intentionally disseminated to others may provide a cause for litigation. There are two types: *libel* and *slander*. **Libel** is the written word defaming another, while **slander** is the publication by any other means.

E. A Park Officer's Immunities to Liability

As a park ranger or park police officer, what protections do I have from exposure to liability?

In addition to some of the issues already discussed above, the following protections should be mentioned:

1. *Good faith*: An individual performing responsibilities with good intentions. *Qualified, good-faith immunity* refers to the fact that a person performing in good faith at the "reasonable person" standard or better generally will be found not liable for his or her actions performed within the scope of his or her duties.

2. *Statutory relief*: An act granting relief or limits on liability may occur in some jurisdictions to protect certain activities of law enforcement officers.

3. *Governmental (or Sovereign) Immunity*: The common law immunity, which has been abolished or narrowed in all jurisdictions of the United States. Most states and the United States have tort claims acts allowing individuals to seek relief or restitution from the government.

4. *Information and Training*: Probably the most effective defense against liability is proactive. This includes adequate training, continual maintenance of skills and current information relating to one's duties and responsibilities. As an example, a ranger performing within the reasonable standards of the profession will normally avoid engaging in activities that produce harm.

5. *Insurance*: Liability insurance can be invaluable. It will allow the ranger to work in good faith without fear of serious repercussions.

NOTES

CHAPTER XIX

SPECIAL TOPICS IN LIABILITY:

TRAINING, DRIVING UNDER THE INFLUENCE ENFORCEMENT, AND RIDE-ALONG PROGRAMS

A. Liability in Law Enforcement Training

One of the growing liability areas in law enforcement concerns the notion of **training negligence.** The courts have held that under certain circumstances, the victim of some police abuse, misconduct or other action may take civil action against the officer and his or her entity if the officer's behavior is a product of negligent training. This type of suit often involves civil rights law (i.e., 42 USC §1983) but could also stem from other liability avenues.

What makes law enforcement training "negligent"?

Whether or not training is negligent is determined on a case-by-case basis. In general, it would have to be demonstrated that the training does not meet currently acceptable standards within the law enforcement training community, omits important aspects, is not adequately documented, is not taught by experts in their fields, or contains inadequate standards for the trainee's successful completion. Like many areas of the law, the standards for training negligence are still evolving; thus, the prudent law enforcement manager, trainer or practitioner would be well advised to take a proactive approach toward the issue and insure that law enforcement training and in-service training programs are professionally conducted.

What can I expect to face in training negligence litigation?

There is no way to predict accurately what will happen in any given courtroom when you are facing litigation over law enforcement training practices. Nor is it even possible to determine whether the matter will be resolved out of court. In general, however, you can expect that the plaintiff's attorney has researched the particular area of training that is at issue. He or she has gone to established experts in that particular type of training and discovered what the "state of the art" is with respect to the issue at hand. The attorney will utilize the process of discovery which will include questioning you and others outside of court before trial and will subpoena your training records.

What specific steps can I take to reduce my exposure to liability related to training practices?

Although this question cannot be answered completely, the following guidelines will help trainers to evaluate their programs and trainees to assess the training in which they are asked to participate.

1. Is there a complete course syllabus and lesson plan which you can produce on demand?
2. Are there complete attendance records on every student in every class which you can produce on demand?
3. Are the instructors experts in the areas they have been assigned to instruct? Can you document their expertise?
4. Are the resource materials, books, and training aids current, appropriate, and related?
5. Where special instructor certifications are generally the norm (e.g., firearms, CPR, etc.), do the instructors hold them?
6. Are copies of the course quizzes and exams available for inspection?
7. Are records of each student's performance available for each testing situation?
8. Do the testing procedures preclude cheating?
9. In firearms training, do the trainees qualify
   a) with the particular weapon(s) they carry?
   b) with the particular ammunition they carry?

c) with their weapons under reduced illumination as well as in daylight?
d) within the times allowed by the timed courses of fire (i.e., or are they allowed to shoot "alibis")?
e) with a shotgun, if they have access to one?

10. Has the program ever failed a student? If not, how are you going to demonstrate that the program maintains any standards?

11. To what extent is the purported length of the program inflated in terms of the actual number of training hours given?

12. Does the program contain any role-play or situation training component through which you have an opportunity to assess students' interpersonal and technical skills as they attempt to apply them in law enforcement settings?

13. Do you and your trainers understand the importance of identifying and reporting any trainees who, because of their behavior, lead you to believe that they possess personality traits that make them unsuited for the law enforcement role (e.g., tempers, racism, etc.)?

14. If you are employing officers who were trained by someone other than yourself, have you investigated the training program and are you satisfied that it meets all the above standards?

15. Do you provide for periodic in-service law enforcement training programs, and does the content of these programs address perceived needs or inadequacies that may arise among your law enforcement personnel?

What these 15 areas amount to is a checklist against training negligence. Clearly, a potential avenue for a plaintiff to get into the "deep pockets" of a park agency is to maintain that the mistreatment, injury, or loss he or she received from one of its officers resulted in part from incompetent or inadequate law enforcement training and supervision. An effective training program can minimize this threat.

B. Managing the Intoxicated Driver

A question often facing park rangers is what to do with drivers who have been drinking alcoholic beverages. Should they be arrested and transported to jail? Should they be driven home? Should they be told to park by the side of the road for an hour to sober up? Should a sober occupant of the vehicle be identified and given responsibility for driving it? What if a person under the influence is stopped and released? What is the liability picture if such a driver subsequently inflicts injury to him- or herself or to a third party?

Although the law is still evolving on this point, under some circumstances it may be possible to hold an officer liable for injury or loss sustained by a third party who was injured by an intoxicated driver who was stopped by the officer shortly before, but allowed to continue driving.

What is the "Public Duty" Doctrine?

The public duty doctrine holds that an officer's duty is to the general public and not to any specific person, unless a "special duty" has been created.

Doesn't this doctrine protect me from liability resulting from a third party injured by a drunk driver whom I have previously stopped and released?

It is true that this doctrine implies that the failure to restrain an intoxicated driver, where the driver subsequently causes harm to a third party, allows the third party no cause of action. The law enforcement officer's historical duty is to the general public and not to a specific individual; however, this duty is being redefined and expanded in the courts. In some of the cases dealing with the failure to restrain, the courts decided in favor of the public duty doctrine, maintaining that a duty to the individual plaintiff did not exist.

In other cases, however, the doctrine was set aside and the officers or their entities were found liable. The courts' reasoning in some cases favoring the plaintiff held that a special duty to protect individuals from drunk drivers was created by statutes spelling out police duties to enforce drunk driving laws.

How do the concepts of discretionary and ministerial function apply to the release of intoxicated drivers?

Discretion (discussed earlier) may be defined as "the power to act within general guidelines, rules, or laws, but without either specific rules to follow or the need to completely explain or justify each decision or action." *Ministerial* implies that acts are done by carrying out orders rather than by making choices of how to act. *Ministerial functions* are activities that are absolute, fixed and certain, and in the performance of which there is no discretion. They are done by carrying out a general policy rather than by setting or making policy.

Because officers, and their entities, are traditionally immune to liability stemming from discretionary acts, the outcome of a case may center on whether the court considers an officer's decision to arrest a drunk driver to be discretionary, denying liability, or ministerial, implying liability.

What is the best alternative when I stop a driver whom I consider too intoxicated to drive?

In general, the best alternative is to arrest the driver and transport him or her to jail. This strategy precludes the possibility of the driver harming him- or herself or someone else. Of course, any given situation may call for a different solution, but you should be aware that it may also create a potential for greater liability frontage.

C. Liability and Ride-Along Programs

Many parks are faced with requests from non-commissioned park employees as well as from members of the public to ride along with a patrol ranger during his or her tour of duty. Also, occasions may arise when park administration invites various members of the public to ride along with a patrol ranger or other park law enforcement officer. These situations often create questions for managers regarding liability, should the passenger become injured as a result of the activity.

What must I do to reduce liability exposure in these ride-along situations?

a. Ride-along programs should require that such passengers accompany only experienced rangers possessing good skills, techniques, and judgment.

b. Legal expertise should be consulted to develop a *hold-harmless agreement* (release) to mitigate any damages ensuing from an incident. The agreement should include acknowledgement of the potential harms that may be encountered in the company of a park law enforcement officer, as well as a statement clearly intending to hold harmless the ranger, supervisors, and entity in the event of an incident. It should be recognized that, although they are recommended, hold-harmless agreements are of limited value.

c. As a rule, it is wise for the entity to acquire insurance to cover potential damages and litigation expenses.

NOTES

CHAPTER XX

SOME LEGAL ASPECTS OF DRUG ENFORCEMENT

How would I know that my park has a drug problem that should be addressed?

There are several possible indiccators:
1. incidents of drug overdoses
2. incidents of drug-related violence
3. identification of individuals clearly under the influence
4. reports from local and state narcotics officers that the park is used as a transaction area
5. discovery by park employees of drug paraphernalia
6. discovery of marijuana plants growing on park property
7. observations of probable drug transactions between visitors
8. reports from the public and park neighbors that drug use is occurring in the park

What strategies are available for managing a park drug problem?

There are fundamentally only two strategies available to the parks for carrying out such a mission: (1) The first approach is to discover the source of the drugs and attempt to reduce the supply to the visitors or employees by identifying the producers and dealers and interdicting the transportation and supply. (2) The second approach is to target the users or buyers of illegal drugs and to intervene in a way that will reduce the likelihood that they will use or purchase drugs again in the park. For either of the above approaches, some covert activities will probably be necessary to accomplish the mission.

What techniques are available to target the dealers and/or users of illegal drugs?

One technique would entail the use of undercover officers "hanging around" likely locations for drug activity, perhaps attempting to buy drugs from suspected dealers, keeping notes, and possibly seeking warrants for any dealers who may be identified. The problem with arresting any given drug dealer is that the drug-dealing niche he or she has occupied will immediately be filled by some other dealer.

A second approach incorporates the technique known as the **reverse sting.** In reverse stings, park officers or informants posing as drug dealers make drug sales and then, together with backup undercover officers in the immediate area, arrest the buyers. To maximize safety, these teams are carefully trained and follow a highly structured procedure for making contacts with potential buyers, completing a sale, and then effecting an arrest. Each team member has a specific job to do and acts in total coordination with the other members. Procedures for these activities have been worked out and field tested by numerous law enforcement agencies.

Is it legal for law enforcement officers to sell drugs?

This question has been addressed many times and legal opinions and case law indicate that the answer is "yes." 21 U.S.C. § 841(a) makes it a federal offense to distribute a controlled substance. However, it is generally held that an officer is not criminally liable in this situation because his or her behavior lacks the necessary element of criminal intent. In addition to the legal tradition that would exempt an officer who sells illegal drugs in a reverse sting, federal drug law exists that specifically provides this immunity in 21 U.S.C. § 855(d).

Can reverse sting operations be considered entrapment?

Entrapment occurs when a law enforcement official plants in the mind of an otherwise innocent person the inclination to engage in a criminal act. Merely providing the opportunity to engage in a criminal act, however, does not constitute entrapment.

In the implementation of successful reverse stings, *predisposition* of the potential defendant will remain the critical element should he or she, when prosecuted, claim entrapment. To avoid a court ruling that the ranger overstepped his or her duties by inciting or creating the crime, the ranger should remain a neutral salesman and allow the buyer's predisposition to control the transaction. It may be considered entrapment for the law enforcement officer to encourage or lure a customer with overly zealous selling techniques into buying something the customer doesn't want.

What are some guidelines for reducing the risk of entrapment?

1. When officer-sellers solicit business, they should not mention words such as "crack," "coke," "dope," "grass," "ice," or any other illegal drug.

2. Officers should not attempt to encourage a person to buy from them if, at first, he or she denies interest in a drug purchase.

3. Specific people should not be selected for an extra intensive selling effort. The courts have held that targeting specific individuals for sting activities requires a reasonable suspicion that they are likely to engage in the crime. Remember, in the type of "reverse-sting" operation being discussed here, it is not the individual as much as the activity that is being targeted.

What steps are involved in setting up a reverse-sting drug operation?

1. First, it may be necessary to educate those in authority about reverse stings and explain their value in addressing the issue of drug abuse at the particular park site. Such an attempt will probably include reassurances about the legal aspects of reverse stings, as well as reassurances regarding the public relations implications of such programs.
2. Similarly, the local court and prosecutors with whom the park works will have to be brought into the planning discussions.

3. Other area law enforcement agencies should also be contacted and brought into the planning. One valuable strategy (where jurisdictions overlap) is to involve some of these other officers in the reverse stings, thus taking advantage of their experience and sharing with them and their agencies the kudos associated with such undertakings.

4. Where feasible, trustworthy sources in the local media can be contacted and briefed on the plan so that when it is put into operation, there is an increased potential for effective, positive press coverage of what the park is trying to accomplish.

5. The selection of the reverse-sting team is clearly a critical component to the program's success. Reverse stings are highly orchestrated operations in which every participant knows exactly what his or her role will be. Each position has a specific name and associated responsibility, and there is a "play-book" by which everyone functions. Members should be volunteers who are physically in shape and adequately trained in self defense and arrest techniques.

6. The reverse-sting team must undergo an adequate amount of briefing and scenario training to give the members experience with what they are going to say, how they are going to act as a team, and what they will do should unique types of situations arise. It is wise to videotape this training to provide additional feedback to the participants.

7. With respect to the drugs that will be sold, decisions have to be made as to their type and sources of supply have to be obtained. Although the particular drugs employed may vary from area to area, most sellers will probably find that it will be necessary to provide cocaine, crack cocaine, and marijuana. With the approval of the court, arrangements can be made through local, state, and federal narcotics enforcement to obtain the drugs. Of course, an accounting system will have to be established.

8. In situations in which buyers use motor vehicles to arrive at the selling site, these vehicles may be confiscated. As part of the reverse-sting planning, a procedure (manpower) will be necessary for removing these vehicles from the scene.

9. Locations for potential reverse stings must be identified and evaluated for their appropriateness. Such factors as exposure to the public, possible escape routes, locations for back-up positioning, and personal safety of the officers, the buyers, and the visiting public must all be taken into account and incorporated into the plan. Also, intelligence must be gathered as to the typical *modus operandi* of drug dealers in the area so these strategies may be duplicated.

NOTES

GLOSSARY

Accessory After the Fact: An accessory after the fact knows that the felony has been committed and gives aid and comfort to the felons by assisting in their escape, or their avoiding detection or arrest.

Accessory Before the Fact: An accessory before the fact is a person who aids, counsels, directs, or orders the commission of a crime but is not present at the time the actual crime is committed. These persons may also be principals in the second degree.

Adult: A person who has reached his eighteenth birthday, unless declared otherwise by law.

Affidavit: A sworn statement.

Arraignment: The accused is called before the court to hear the formal charges against him and enter a plea.

Arrest: Taking a person into custody or depriving a person of the freedom to come and go because he is a suspect in a particular crime.

Assault: A threat to do bodily harm.

Attempt: An attempt to commit a crime is the action of preparation, but just falling short of completion. An attempted murder may involve injury but does not result in death.

Bail: A sum of money set by the judge to insure that the accused will show up and submit to trial.

Battery: The unlawful touching of another, frequently used with assault.

Bench Warrant: A warrant issued from the bench (i.e., a judge in court).

Burden of Proof: The responsibility of the prosecution to prove the accusation with sufficient evidence and, in a criminal case, to establish guilt beyond a reasonable doubt.

Chain of Custody: The protected and documented progression of evidence from the time it is seized until it is admitted at trial. An adequate chain of custody insures the trustworthiness of the evidence.

Change of Venue: The transfer of a court case from one location, such as a county, to another. The motion is made where it appears the venue location is prejudicial or inflamed and the defendant would be denied a fair trail.

Charge: The accusation for which a person is held and tried.

Civil Action: A civil, as opposed to criminal, legal proceeding in which a party seeks some remedy such as money, damages or an injunction.

Color of Law: The figurative cloak or mantle of authority of a public official to carry out the functions of his or her office. It allows a person to act in an official capacity.

Common Law: The law that is derived from the historical customs and court decisions based on those customs as opposed to statutory law.

Competency: The judge will determine the fitness of a witness to testify in a trial or the fitness of documentary or physical evidence to be admitted.

Competent: In criminal matters, the ability to understand the nature and seriousness of the charges and the ability to assist in one's defense.

Complaint: A sworn statement alleging a crime by a particular person.

Conduct: Conduct, in the eyes of the law, includes acts and failure to act.

Consent: A waiver of a constitutional right given with the knowledge of the right not to do so. It must be given freely, intelligently, and without coercion.

Conspiracy: An agreement between two or more people to commit a crime.

Contemporaneous: Occurring at the same time and place.

Contempt of Court: Willful disobedience of a court order.

Continuance: The postponement of a court proceeding to a later date.

Contraband: Property that may not be lawfully possessed and may be lawfully taken by an officer for that reason. This does not normally include real estate.

***Corpus Delicti*:** The object upon which the crime was committed, such as the body of a murder victim or the shell of a boat that was burned.

Credibility: The jury's decision of whether a witness is credible, believable.

Criminal Intent: The criminal intention to knowingly and willfully engage in the criminal act, which is required to establish guilt. Reckless conduct may suffice to demonstrate intent, as may negligent behavior.

Cross-Examination: The in-court questioning of a witness for the opposition to determine the truthfulness and accuracy of the testimony that he or she gave.

Curtilage: The close space around a dwelling that is considered part of the dwelling and is the premises in which there is the highest reasonable expectation of privacy. It is the space that would be found within the "picket fence," and includes close out buildings in which a man or woman could stand, such as a barn, corn crib, chicken house, etc.

Damages: The money compensation awarded the plaintiff in a civil action for an injury or loss. Compensatory damages are for the actual loss or injury, while the punitive damages are over and above that amount to punish the offender and deter repetition of the harmful act.

Delinquent: A juvenile who has committed a crime.

Detention: The temporary holding of a person for the purpose of investigation. The action is for a very short period and does not constitute an arrest.

Double Jeopardy: The United States Constitution prohibition of the prosecution of a person for the same crime by the same jurisdiction more than once unless the matter is appealed by the accused.

Dual Sovereignty: The situation in which a crime offends more than one jurisdiction (sovereign), such as federal and state and either or both could prosecute without violating prohibitions of double jeopardy.

Due Process: The constitutionally guaranteed protections and procedures preventing loss of life, liberty, or property without such proper legal safeguards.

D.U.I.: Driving under the influence, i.e., being under the influence of some intoxicant or drug.

D.W.I.: Driving while intoxicated, which in most jurisdictions is driving while intoxicated by some drug or alcohol. With alcohol, it is generally a blood level of at least 0.1% by weight.

Elements of a Crime: Certain elements which must be proven to convict a person of any particular crime. As an example, the elements of burglary (common law or first degree in most states) are the (1) breaking and (2) entering, of the (3) dwelling of (4) another (5) at night, with the (6) intention of committing a felony. All of the elements must be proven plus the fact that the accused did the acts at the time and place stated.

Elephant Rule: The area in which an officer may search, which is confined to the place of need or the place where the item sought is likely to be. If searching for an elephant, you may not look in the glove compartment. If you are searching for narcotics, on the other hand, a glove compartment would probably be an appropriate place to look.

Entrapment: The defense that the accused did the act but that the only reason was that the law enforcement officer tricked or persuaded him to do so. The theory is that the evil intent originated in the mind of the officer who was trying to entrap the accused.

Evidence: The testimony or tangible objects introduced in a trial to convince the jury or judge of the truth of a fact at issue.

Exclusionary Rule: A judicially created rule that allows the defendant or court to suppress (exclude) for trial any evidence, or derivatives thereof, obtained illegally by governmental officers or agents acting under color of law.

Exigent Circumstances: Unusual circumstances allowing quick action where such is not normally permitted. A scream, a shot, the probability that evidence is about to be destroyed immediately, the presence of great immediate danger, etc. are examples.

Ex Post Facto: The United States Constitution prohibition of an action being made a crime after it occurs. It also prohibits the increasing of a penalty for the crime after the act.

Extenuating Circumstances: Facts concerning the commission of a crime that may reduce the punishment. This does not excuse the crime; it may only lessen the penalty.

Extradition: The legal process by which one jurisdiction obtains a person for prosecution from another jurisdiction holding the person.

False Arrest: The unlawful detention or holding of a person.

Felony: A serious crime for which the punishment is normally a year or more in prison.

Frisk: A pat down of outer clothing for the purpose of looking for weapons and based on the belief that the suspect may be armed or dangerous. The pat down includes all external clothing and is not a search.

Fruits of a Crime: Items gained from the commission of a crime, e.g., money from the bank robbery.

Fruit of the Poisonous Tree: Otherwise legal and proper evidence obtained as the product of other illegal police activity which is not, as a rule, admissible.

Grand Jury: A group of citizens taken from a cross section of a community by law to hear the presentation of some evidence in a case and determine if there is sufficient probable cause to indict. If the Grand Jury determines that there is sufficient probable cause it hands down an indictment.

Habeas Corpus: A petition by one who believes that he is being held in jail illegally and demanding that the holding authority justify the detention or release him.

Had Reason to Know: An individual, normally a defendant, had such information that a person of at least reasonable intelligence would derive that a particular fact exists.

Harm: When considering liability, a measurable injury to a person, property, or interest.

Hearsay: A statement by one witness of what he heard another person say.

Indictment: The formal written charges against an individual on which the person is brought to trial. The indictment is handed down by the Grand Jury.

Initial Appearance: The first judicial hearing for the accused for the purpose of determining detention, bond or both.

Injury: In discussing liability, an injury is some type of intrusion upon an interest protected by tort law.

Insane: A legal term dealing with the suspect's mental state at the time the offense was committed. A person may be found not guilty by reason of insanity. The theory holds that the insane person's mental state prevented his having the evil intent to commit the act.

Intoxication: Having one's behavior influenced by some chemical such as alcohol. Normally, voluntary intoxication is not a defense to a crime.

Judicial Notice: The judge taking notice of a fact without its having to be proved (e.g., it is dark at midnight).

"Jump and Reach" Rule: The search area immediately around the arrestee where the person in custody might "jump and reach" a weapon or destroy evidence.

Jurisdiction: The authority to inquire into a crime, deal with it through arrest and trial, and pass sentence.

Juvenile: A person who has not reached his eighteenth birthday, unless declared otherwise by law.

Mala in Se: Crimes which are naturally wrong in themselves such as murder, rape, kidnapping, burglary and robbery.

Mala Prohibita: Crimes created by law which are wrong because the acts impose on others or interfere with the orderly operation of society. Examples would be: speeding, illegal parking, and walking on the grass.

Malice: The criminal intent or state of mind causing the person to commit the crime.

Mere Suspicion: A hunch, or a feeling based on the officer's experience that something is amiss, which may cause the officer to observe or investigate further. It is not the basis for further action until additional articulable facts elevate the suspicion or knowledge.

Minor: Generally a person who has not reached his eighteenth birthday, unless declared otherwise by law.

Miranda Warning: The Court-mandated warnings that must be given to a suspect prior to in-custody interrogation. These warnings include: (1) the right to remain silent, (2) the right to have an attorney present during interrogation, (3) the right to have a court-appointed attorney if the suspect cannot afford one, and (4) anything the suspect says can be used against him or her in a court of law.

Misdemeanor: A less serious crime for which the punishment is normally less than a year in prison.

Mistrial: A trial which is incomplete because of a deadlocked jury or procedural error. The trial may be held again without double jeopardy interfering.

Modus Operandi, **also M.O.:** The pattern or way of doing something. In criminal matters it normally refers to the pattern of committing the crime by a particular individual or group.

Moving Roadblock: An officer on patrol stopping vehicles or persons in vehicles matching a particular description or a particular need such as permit checks, license checks, etc.

Motive: The reason a person committed the crime.

Negligence: An act or omission of an act that causes harm to another which the reasonably prudent person would not do. This occurs in criminal and civil matters.

Open Fields: The areas outside of a curtilage in which an owner's expectation of privacy is diminished.

Perjury: A statement made under oath in a judicial proceeding, which the person making the statement knows to be false.

Physical harm: In liability, a term which implies abuse of the person or property of another.

Plaintiff: The party bringing suit in a civil action.

Plain View: Items which an officer may observe without moving objects or entering an area in which he or she does not have a right to be. Objects may be observed with the aid of a flashlight, binoculars, etc.

Plea: The accused enters a plea before trial, normally guilty or not guilty or *nolo contendre*. A plea of "guilty" is a total admission to all of the facts of the charge to which it is entered. A "not guilty" plea is a total denial of all facts. The *"nolo contendre"* is a denial for civil purposes but an admission for criminal purposes (I didn't do it and I won't do it again).

Preliminary Hearing: A judicial hearing to determine probable cause to hold an accused and set bail.

Presumption: An inference at law that a fact exists because of another fact.

Presumption of Innocence: A presumption that all persons are innocent even though charged with a crime. This presumption lasts throughout the trial process until the jury returns a verdict of guilty. The state must overcome this presumption by proving beyond a reasonable doubt that the accused committed the particular crime as charged.

Principal: Principals are designated principals in the first or second degree. A principal in the first degree is the person who actually commits the crime. If more than one person commits the crime, all are principals in the first degree. A principal in the second degree is normally absent at the time the crime is committed but aids in the actual commission.

Probable Cause: In arrest, the existence of more reason to believe than not that a particular person committed a particular crime.

Reasonable Suspicion: The belief by an experienced reasonable officer that a crime is about to be, is being, or has been committed (short of probable cause to support an arrest) which gives the officer the grounds to stop, and frisk if appropriate, an individual for a brief investigative time to determine the circumstances and determine if probable cause does in fact exist.

Search Warrant: A court order directing an officer to search a specified location, person or object for particular evidence of a suspected crime and to seize such evidence if it is found.

Self Defense: The defense in a court proceeding that the accused had to use the force in question to defend himself and that he had a right to do so.

Search (of a person): A search conducted pursuant to a warrant and within the scope of the warrant or incident to an arrest. The search incident to arrest is to protect the officer, prevent the destruction of evidence, and prevent escape or suicide.

Search (of an area): The search for particular evidence, contraband, fruits, or instrumentalities of a crime pursuant to (a) a warrant and within the scope and time frame of the warrant, or (b) a search of the immediate surrounding area ("jump and reach" rule) of an arrestee, which is permitted pursuant to the arrest if contemporaneous in time and place.

Should have Known: An aspect of negligence, which holds that a person of reasonable intelligence would know of a particular fact or set of facts and govern his or her behavior accordingly.

Specific Intent: The requirement in some crimes of the proof of specific intent to commit the crime or cause the result, which cannot be presumed from the unlawful act itself.

Statute: Laws enacted by the legislative body and signed into law by the presiding executive, governor, or president.

Statute of Limitations: A statutory creation of a time limit in which an indictment must be filed or the crime may not be prosecuted. Statutes of limitation vary from one jurisdiction to another, but as a rule the more serious crimes are not included and may be prosecuted at any time.

Subpoena: An order of the court commanding the appearance of a person to give testimony and to bring certain objects if so ordered.

Suppression Hearing: A judicial hearing to determine whether or not evidence should be suppressed under the Exclusionary Rule because the evidence is incompetent.

"Terry" Frisk: A frisk that had judicial approval in the case *Terry v. Ohio*; that is, a pat down of outer clothing for the purpose of looking for weapons and based on the belief that the suspect may be armed or dangerous. The pat down includes all external clothing and is not a search. See cases for further information.

Tort: A wrongful act or failure to act which causes injury or loss to another and for which the injured party may sue for damages or injunction.

Unruly Behavior: Behavior peculiar to juveniles that is contrary to law, such as: drinking, smoking, being out after curfew, etc.

Venire: The group of citizens from which a jury is drawn.

Venue: The location or site of the crime.

Verdict: A finding by the judge or jury after all of the evidence has been presented.

VIN: Vehicle Identification Number. A number required by law and normally on a plate assigned to a particular vehicle. The number is easily observed and accessible to view and, if covered, may be cleared for viewing by the officer.

RELEVANT LEGAL CASES

ARRESTS

Warrantless Arrests

Payton v. New York, 445 U.S. 573, 100 S.Ct. 1371, 63 L.Ed. 2d 639 (1980): The Fourth Amendment prohibits police from making a warrantless and non-consensual entry into a suspect's home (or premises) in order to make a routine felony arrest. Entry may be made without a warrant only if the officer is in hot pursuit or there are exigent circumstances.

United States v. Watson, 423 U.S. 411, 96 S.Ct. 820, 46 L.Ed.2d 598 (1976): Failure to secure a warrant for an arrest will not invalidate the arrest if it is based on probable cause.

California v. Hodari D., ___ U.S. ___, 111 S.Ct. 1547, 113 L.Ed.2d 690 (1991): In order for a seizure of the person to have occurred, there must be either some application of physical force, even if extremely slight, or a show of authority to which the subject submits. A show of authority, without any application of physical force and to which the subject does not yield, is not a "seizure."

Hearings

County of Riverside v. McLaughlin, ___ U.S. ___, 111 S.Ct. 1661, 114 L.Ed.2d 49 (1991): A jurisdiction that has probable cause determination must do so as soon as reasonably feasible, but no more than 48 hours after the arrest.

BAIL:

Stack v. Boyle, 342 U.S. 1, 72 S.Ct. 1, 96 L.Ed. 3 (1951): Bail is excessive if it exceeds the amount necessary to insure the accused's presence at trial.

COUNSEL:

Brewer v. Williams, 430 U.S. 387, 97 S.Ct. 1232, 51 L.Ed.2d 424 (1977): The police may not interrogate once an accused has refused to speak without his attorney being present.

Brown v. Mississippi, 297 U.S. 278, 56 S.Ct. 461, 80 L.Ed. 682 (1936): Confessions obtained by coercion are a violation of due process.

Escobedo v. Illinois, 378 U.S. 478, 84 S.Ct. 1758, 12 L.Ed.2d 977 (1964): Incriminating statements made during an interrogation in which requests for counsel were denied and Miranda warnings were not given are inadmissible at trial.

Gideon v. Wainwright, 372 U.S. 335, 83 S.Ct. 792, 9 L.Ed.2d 799 (1963): An accused is entitled to counsel in a trial.

Massiah v. United States, 377 U.S. 201, 84 S.Ct. 1199, 12 L.Ed.2d 246 (1964): An accused's incriminating words obtained after charges had been filed during an interrogation without benefit of counsel may not be introduced against him in trial.

Spano v. New York, 360 U.S. 315, 79 S.Ct. 1202, 3 L.Ed.2d 1265 (1959): A confession obtained through fatigue and sympathy is involuntary and inadmissible.

DEADLY FORCE:

Tennessee v. Garner, 475 U.S.1, 105 S.Ct. 1694, 85 L.Ed.2d 1 (1985): Deadly force may not be used to effect an arrest. Deadly force may be used only where the officer has reason to believe that the suspect poses a significant threat of death or serious injury to the officer or to others.

ELECTRONIC SURVEILLANCE, INFORMANTS, AND AGENTS:

Hoffa v. United States, 385 U.S. 293, 87 S.Ct. 408, 17 L.Ed.2d 374 (1966): Evidence obtained from a secret informer is valid if the evidence is given voluntarily and based on "misplaced confidence."

Katz v. United States, 389 U.S. 347, 88 S.Ct. 507, 19 L.Ed.2d 576 (1967): A person with a reasonable expectation of privacy is protected by the Fourth Amendment, and a physical trespass without a warrant is a breach of that privacy.

Lewis v. United States, 385 U.S. 206, 87 S.Ct. 424, 17 L.Ed.2d 312 (1966): An agent, under cover, may deceptively enter a premises that has become a commercial center (i.e., selling narcotics) without a warrant and all observations and conversations are legal seizures.

United States v. White, 401 U.S. 745, 91 S.Ct. 1122, 28 L.Ed.2d 453 (1971): The Fourth Amendment does not apply where a person voluntarily confides wrongdoing. A person's expectations of trust are not protected.

ENTRAPMENT:

United States v. Russell, 411 U.S. 423, 93 S.Ct. 1637, 36 L.Ed.2d 366 (1973): The question of entrapment is for the jury, which will assess the defendant's predisposition to commit a crime rather than the type or degree of police conduct.

EXCLUSIONARY RULE:

Mapp v. Ohio: 367 U.S. 643, 81 S.Ct. 1684, 6 L.Ed.2d 1081 (1961): Affirmed the Exclusionary Rule; evidence obtained improperly (in this case, without a valid search warrant) may not be used against a defendant in court.

Segura v. United States, 468 U.S. 796, 104 S.Ct. 3380, 82 L.Ed.2d 599 (1984): The Exclusionary Rule does not apply if the connection between illegal police conduct, discovery, and the resultant seizure of evidence is so "attenuated as to dissipate the taint."

FIRST AMENDMENT:

A Quaker Action Group v. Morton, 516 F.2d 717 (1975): Although some parks may be reserved for specific purposes, in general, public assembly for First Amendment purposes is a justifiable "park use."

GOOD FAITH:

Malley v. Briggs, 475 U.S. 335, 106 S.Ct. 1092, 89 L.Ed.2d 271 (1986): Explored limits of qualified good-faith immunity to alleged Fourth Amendment violations. Even though he had a warrant, the officer was liable for an unconstitutional arrest because he should have known that the facts presented for the warrant did not establish probable cause. The officer must exercise reasonable professional judgment.

SELECTED FIFTH AMENDMENT CASES

Coercion

Arizona v. Fulminante, ___ U.S. ___, 111 S.Ct. 1246, 113 L.Ed.2d 302 (1991): Whether or not a confession is coerced depends on the totality of the circumstances; if, however, a defendant's confession is coerced, its use against the defendant will be reviewed from the beginning (*de novo*) under the harmless error rule.

Informing Suspects of Their Rights

Beckwith v. United States, 425 U.S. 341, 96 S.Ct. 1612, 48 L.Ed.2d 1 (1976): Miranda is not applicable to a non-custodial interrogation that is voluntary in nature.

Berkemer v. McCarty, 468 U.S. 420, 104 S.Ct. 3138, 82 L.Ed.2d 317 (1984): Before questioning, Miranda warnings must be given to a suspect taken into custody, even for a traffic violation.

Colorado v. Spring, 479 U.S. 564, 107 S.Ct. 851, 93 L.Ed.2d 954 (1987): As long as they are Mirandized, subjects of custodial interrogation do not have to be informed in advance of the subject of the interrogation.

Illinois v. Perkins, ___ U.S. ___, 110 S.Ct. 2394, 110 L.Ed. 2d 243 (1990): A law enforcement officer posing as an inmate need not uncover his or her identity by giving Miranda warnings to a jail suspect before asking questions that may elicit an incriminating response regarding an uncharged crime.

Miranda v. Arizona: 384 U.S. 436, 86 S.Ct. 1602, 16 L.Ed.2d 694 (1966): Established the standard for advising suspects of their constitutional right to counsel and against self incrimination before any custodial interrogation by law enforcement officers takes place. The warning is to include the fact that the accused will have counsel appointed for him at no expense to himself if he cannot afford counsel and that he need not answer questions until he has consulted with counsel.

Moran v. Burbine, 475 U.S.412, 106 S.Ct. 1135, 89 L.Ed.2d 410 (1986), Police have no duty to inform an in-custody suspect about to be questioned that his lawyer is in another room and wants to consult with him.

New York v. Quarles, 467 U.S. 649, 104 S.Ct. 2626, 81 L.Ed.2d 550 (1984): Miranda warnings are not required in urgent or exigent circumstances where there is an overriding concern for public safety.

Oregon v. Elstad, 470 U.S. 298, 105 S.Ct. 1285, 84 L.Ed.2d 222 (1985): After a suspect is informed of the Miranda warnings and makes a voluntary statement, the statement may be used.

Oregon v. Mathiason, 429 U.S. 492, 97 S.Ct. 711, 50 L.Ed.2d 714 (1977): Miranda warnings are required where a suspect has been deprived of his freedom so as to render him in custody, but not for others who may be questioned.

Orozco v. Texas, 394 U.S. 324, 89 S.Ct. 1095, 22 L.Ed.2d 311 (1969): Miranda warnings must be given any time a person is being interrogated and is deprived of his freedom in any way.

Pennsylvania v. Muniz, ___ U.S. ___, 110 S.Ct. 2638, 110 L.Ed. 2d 528 (1990): The absence of Miranda warnings does not prevent the admission, at a drunk driving trial, of the bulk of the video tape recording of the responses and comments uttered by a defendant while he was being tested for sobriety and booked.

Right to Counsel

Mannick v. Mississippi, ___ U.S. ___ 111 S.Ct. 486, 112 L.Ed. 2d 489 (1990): Officials may not reinitiate interrogation of an accused without counsel present after the accused has requested and been provided counsel. The Fifth Amendment protection is not terminated or suspended when the suspect has consulted with an attorney.

INEVITABLE DISCOVERY:

Nix v. Williams, 467 U.S. 431, 104 S.Ct. 2501, 81 L.Ed.2d 377 (1984): Even though evidence would have been suppressed due to a violation of Miranda warnings and lack of counsel, the evidence will not be suppressed when the police did not act in bad faith in a separate search and where it was inevitable that the evidence would be discovered from an independent source.

INVENTORIES:

Colorado v. Bertine, 479 U.S. 367, 107 S.Ct. 738, 93 L.Ed.2d 739 (1987): Inventories of impounded vehicles may include any unsealed container found inside the vehicle, as long as the inventory is done in good faith and not for the purpose of obtaining evidence. Law enforcement officers do not have to offer an arrestee the opportunity to make his or her own arrangements for securing the vehicle; they may impound the vehicle if they wish.

South Dakota v. Opperman, 428 U.S. 364, 96 S.Ct. 3092, 49 L.Ed.2d 100 (1976): A vehicle taken into police custody for protection of the vehicle may be inventoried pursuant to standard police procedures without a warrant.

Florida v. Wells, ___ U.S. ___, 110 S.Ct. 1632, 109 L.Ed.2d 1 (1990): Opening a closed container encountered in a vehicle inventory violates the Fourth Amendment, absent a written policy directing such activity. In no event may the inventory be used as a pretext for uncovering evidence.

JURISDICTION:

Solorio v. U.S., 483 U.S. 435, 107 S.Ct. 2924, 97 L.Ed.2d 364 (1987) The military has jurisdiction over an active duty service member accused of a crime, even if the crime is not service-connected.

LINEUPS:

Kirby v. Illinois, 406 U.S. 682, 92 S.Ct. 1877, 32 L.Ed.2d 411 (1972): There is no right to counsel at a lineup before the accused is arrested or charged.

Neil v. Biggers, 409 U.S. 188, 93 S.Ct. 375, 343 L.Ed.2d 401 (1972): A suspect's rights have been violated and the evidence obtained from a lineup may be excluded when the lineup is unduly suggestive.

United States v. Wade, 388 U.S. 218, 87 S.Ct. 1926, 18 L.Ed.2d 1149 (1967): Once an accused has been formally charged he is entitled to counsel at a lineup.

PROBABLE CAUSE:

Draper v. United States, 358 U.S. 307, 79 S.Ct. 329, 3 L.Ed.2d 327 (1959): Probable cause exists when an officer of reasonable caution believes that an offense is being or is about to be committed, based on objective facts and circumstances.

Illinois v. Gates, 462 U.S. 213, 103 S.Ct. 2317, 76 L.Ed.2d 527 (1983): The rigid "two prong test" is abandoned in favor of the "totality of the circumstances test" when determining whether an informant's tip will support probable cause for the issuance of a search warrant. A warrant may be issued on a partially corroborated anonymous informant's tip.

PROTECTIVE SWEEPS:

Maryland v. Buie, 494 U.S. 325, 110 S.Ct. 1093, 108 L.Ed.2d 276 (1990): Police officers need no more than a reasonable suspicion to conduct a protective "sweep" of a dwelling in which they are making a valid arrest.

SEARCHES:

Consent Searches:

Florida v. Jimeno, ___ U.S. ___, 111 S.Ct. 1801, 114 L.Ed.2d 297 (1991): Consent to search a vehicle extends to closed containers found inside of the vehicle that could contain the object of the search. However, it does not normally extend to locked or sealed containers, unless specifically incorporated in the consent.

Schneckloth v. Bustamonte, 412 U.S. 218, 93 S.Ct. 2041, 36 L.Ed.2d 854 (1973): Consent voluntarily given without coercion will permit a lawful search.

Stoner v. California, 376 U.S. 483, 84 S.Ct. 889, 11 L.Ed.2d 856 (1964): Only persons with actual or apparent authority over the premises may consent to a search of the premises.

Illinois v. Rodriguez, ___ U.S. ___, 110 S.Ct. 2793, 111 L.Ed.2d 148 (1990): The police may enter private premises without a warrant if they are acting in reliance upon the consent of a third party whom they reasonably, but mistakenly, believe has common authority over the premises.

Motor Vehicle Searches:

California v. Acevedo, ___ U.S. ___, 111 S.Ct. 1982, ___ L.Ed.2d ___ (1991): If police have probable cause to believe that a container located within a vehicle contains contraband or evidence, they may search the container, without holding it to procure a search warrant, even if they do not have probable cause to search the vehicle.

Carroll v. United States, 267 U.S. 132, 45 S.Ct. 280, 69 L.Ed. 543 (1925): A warrantless search of an automobile is permissible where there is probable cause to believe the vehicle may be carrying evidence or the fruits or instrumentalities of a crime.

Chambers v. Maroney, 399 U.S. 42, 90 S.Ct. 1975, 26 L.Ed.2d 419 (1970): Affirmed the right of officers to conduct a warrantless search of an arrested person's motor vehicle after it had been towed to the police station.

New York v. Belton, 453 U.S. 454, 101 S.Ct. 2860, 69 L.Ed. 2d 768 (1981): Incident to the lawful arrest of its occupant, the search of a vehicle's interior passenger compartment may include an examination of the contents of any closed or open containers, including the glove compartment, luggage, boxes, bags, clothing, or any other receptacles.

New York v. Class, 475 U.S. 106, 106 S.Ct. 960, 89 L.Ed.2d 81 (1986): There is no reasonable expectation of privacy in a vehicle identification number (VIN).

United States v. Ross, 456 U.S. 798, 102 S.Ct 2157, 72 L.Ed.2d. 572 (1982): A valid warrantless automobile search may, with probable cause, extend to the containers within the vehicle.

Plain View Doctrine

Horton v. California, ___ U.S. ___, 110 S.Ct. 2301, 110 L.Ed.2d 112 (1990): A police officer may make a warrantless seizure of items whose character is "immediately apparent" regardless of whether he had prior reason to believe the items would be encountered. To justify warrantless seizure of an item in plain view, the police officer must not only be lawfully located in a place from which the object can be plainly seen, the officer must also have a lawful right or access to the object itself.

Coolidge v. New Hampshire, 403 U.S. 443, 91 S.Ct. 2022, 29 L.Ed.2d 564 (1971): A valid search warrant is required to search a premises (dwelling) unless there are exigent circumstances. Plain view into a dwelling area is not sufficient for a search.

Arizona v. Hicks, 480 U.S. 321, 107 S.Ct. 1149, 94 L.Ed.2d 347 (1987): Any movement of an object (e.g., turning over piece of electronics to read its serial number) is a "search" and does not come under the "plain view" exception to the warrant requirement.

Premises Searches

Bumper v. North Carolina, 391 U.S. 543, 88 S.Ct. 1788, 20 L.Ed.2d 797 (1968): A search where police gain consensual admission to a premises through deception by claiming to possess a warrant is unlawful.

California v. Greenwood, 486 U.S.35, 108 S.Ct. 1625 (1988): Placing garbage outside the curtilage (e.g., on the curb or in a campground garbage can) results in a loss of a reasonable expectation of privacy with respect to the contents.

United States v. Dunn, 480 U.S. 294, 107 S.Ct. 1134, 94 L.Ed.2d 326 (1987): The Court found four factors to be considered when determining whether an area is within a curtilage: (1) the proximity of the area to the home, (2) whether the area is included in an enclosure around the home, (3) the nature of uses to which area is put, and (4) the steps taken by resident to protect the area from observation by passersby.

United States v. Matlock, 415 U.S. 164, 94 S.Ct. 988, 39 L.Ed.2d 242 (1974): Any person with an equal right to a premises may consent to a search of the premises.

Roadblocks

Michigan v. Sitz, ___ U.S. ___, 110 S.Ct. 2481, 110 L.Ed.2d 412 (1990): Police may employ highway checkpoint stops as a way of detecting and deterring motorists who drive under the influence of intoxicants. Stopping and briefly detaining all motorists passing through such checkpoints is constitutionally reasonable.

Searches Incident to Arrest

Chimel v. California: 395 U.S. 752, 89 S.Ct. 2034, 23 L.Ed.2d 685 (1969): Limited the scope of a search incident to arrest to the area immediately around the arrestee ("jump and reach" rule).

Hudson v. Palmer, 468 U.S. 517, 104 S.Ct. 3194, 82 L.Ed.2d 393 (1984): An incarcerated prisoner does not have a reasonable expectation of privacy and is, therefore, not protected by the Fourth Amendment's protection against unreasonable searches and seizures. A prisoner's clothes could, therefore, be taken for examination, if the prisoner is provided with replacement clothing.

Illinois v. Lafayette, 462 U.S. 640, 103 U.S. 2605, 77 L.Ed.2d 65 (1983): As a part of a routine procedure for admission to confinement, police may search the individual and his or her personal effects if he or she is under lawful arrest.

United States v. Chadwick, 433 U.S. 1, 97 S.Ct. 2476, 53 L.Ed.2d 538 (1977): Sealed containers seized at the time of arrest may not be searched without a warrant.

United States v. Edwards, 415 U.S. 800, 94 S.Ct. 1234, 39 L.Ed.2d 771 (1974): Pursuant to a lawful arrest, clothing worn by the arrestee may be seized as evidence. The arrestee must be given replacement clothing.

United States v. Robinson, 414 U.S. 218, 94 S.Ct. 467, 38 L.Ed.2d 427 (1973): In the case of a lawful, custodial arrest, a full search of the person and objects within his possession is reasonable and proper without a warrant.

Vale v. Louisiana, 399 U.S. 30, 90 S.Ct. 1969, 26 L.Ed.2d 409 (1970): A warrantless search made incident to arrest must be confined to the immediate vicinity of the arrest (jump and reach rule).

Warrant Searches

Davis v. Mississippi, 394 U.S. 721, 89 S.Ct. 1394, 22 L.Ed.2d 676 (1969): Illegally seized evidence is inadmissible at trial.

Hayes v. Florida, 470 U.S. 811, 105 S.Ct. 1643, 84 L.Ed.2d 705 (1985): An individual's Fourth Amendment rights are violated when he is forcibly removed from a place he is entitled to be in order to obtain fingerprints, and the officers are acting without probable cause and judicial supervision.

Massachusetts v. Sheppard, 468 U.S. 981, 104 S.Ct. 3424, 82 L.Ed. 2d 737 (1984): When police officers take every reasonable step to obtain a valid search warrant from a detached, neutral magistrate who assures the officers of the warrant's validity, and when the officers proceed to enforce the warrant, acting in good faith, the evidence will be admissible even though the warrant is subsequently determined to be invalid.

United States v. Leon, 468 U.S. 897, 104 S.Ct. 3405, 82 L.Ed.2d 677 (1984): The Exclusionary Rule does not bar the use of evidence obtained by officers acting in good-faith reasonable reliance on a search warrant issued by a detached and neutral magistrate but ultimately found to be invalid.

Warden v. Hayden, 387 U.S. 294, 87 S.Ct. 1642, 18 L.Ed.2d 782 (1967): A search warrant is the means to search for specific items and does not provide access to a premises to shop for evidence to convict. The duration of the search is for the minimum time to discover the sought items.

Wong Sun v. United States, 371 U.S. 471, 83 S.Ct. 407, 9 L.Ed.2d 441 (1963): Evidence obtained through a lawful search, but based on illegally obtained information or evidence may be excluded as "fruit of the poisonous tree." If the connection between illegal police conduct and the challenged evidence is so removed in time and place or person so as to dissipate the taint, the evidence is admissible.

Warrantless Searches

Andresen v. Maryland, 427 U.S. 463, 96 S.Ct. 2737, 49 L.Ed.2d 627 (1976): The Fifth Amendment protection against self incrimination attaches to the person not to information that may incriminate him.

Cupp v. Murphy, 412 U.S. 291, 93 S.Ct. 2000, 36 L.Ed.2d 900 (1973): Fingernail scrapings taken without consent and absent a formal arrest are constitutional.

Dunaway v. New York, 442 U.S. 200, 99 S.Ct. 2248, 60 L.Ed.2d 824 (1979): The Fourth Amendment is violated when a person is taken into custody, detained and questioned without probable cause. Evidence obtained from such a custodial questioning is inadmissible.

Minnesota v. Olson, ____ U.S. ____, 110 S.Ct. 1684, 109 L.Ed. 2d 85 (1990): A guest in a home has a legitimate expectation of privacy in the residence and is, therefore, entitled to the protection of the Fourth Amendment against police intrusion on that interest.

Schmerber v. California, 384 U.S. 757, 86 S.Ct. 1826, 16 L.Ed.2d 908 (1966): Where evidence in the blood could be destroyed by delay, a warrant is not necessary to take a blood sample. The Fifth Amendment prohibition on self incrimination applies only to items of a testimonial nature.

United States v. Dionisio, 410 U.S. 1, 93 S.Ct. 764, 35 L.Ed. 2d 67 (1973): Non-testimonial evidence is not protected by the Fourth Amendment's prohibition against unreasonable searches and seizures. Examples of non-testimonial evidence include such things as: fingerprinting, photographing, measurements, requests to write or speak for identification, stand, assume a stance, to engage in a particular task, make a particular gesture, or appear in a lineup.

STOP AND FRISK

Adams v. Williams, 407 U.S. 143, 92 S.Ct. 1921, 32 L.Ed.2d 612 (1972): An informant's tip may be sufficient for a stop and frisk even though it would be inadequate to support an arrest warrant. The officer must have a reasonable belief that criminal activity is afoot and the informant's tip must bear some indication of reliability.

Alabama v. White, ___ U.S. ___, 110 S.Ct. 2412, 110 L. Ed. 2d 301 (1990): The combination of an anonymous tip, which alleged that the defendant was about to transport cocaine in a car, and a police officer's corroboration of some of the tip's details provided reasonable suspicion for stopping the vehicle.

Brown v. Texas: 443 U.S. 47, 99 S.Ct. 2637, 61 L.Ed.2d 357 (1979): A person may not be forcibly stopped for mere suspicion. He may be stopped for reasonable (articulable) suspicion.

Terry v. Ohio: 392 U.S. 1, 88 S.Ct. 1868, 20 L.Ed.2d 889 (1968): Established the right of law enforcement officers to stop and frisk individuals whom they reasonably suspect of being involved in criminal activity and that they believe may be armed and dangerous.

United States v. Sharpe, 470 U.S. 675 105 S.Ct. 1568, 84 L.Ed.2d 605 (1985): A suspect may be detained for a brief period while officers conduct an investigation, provided the officers' actions are justified and limited to the needs under the circumstances.

SURVEILLANCE

California v. Ciraolo, 476 U.S. 207, 106 S.Ct. 1809, 90 L.Ed.2d 210 (1986): There is no reasonable expectation of privacy from aerial surveillance, even within a curtilage.

Oliver v. United States, 466 U.S. 170, 104 S.Ct. 1735, 80 L.Ed.2d 214 (1984): Open fields do not provide the setting for those intimate activities that the Fourth Amendment is intended to protect from governmental interference or surveillance. The Fourth Amendment does not protect merely subjective expectations of privacy, but only those expectations that society is prepared to recognize as reasonable.

THE CONSTITUTION OF THE UNITED STATES

SELECTED AMENDMENTS

from

THE BILL OF RIGHTS
(AMENDMENTS 1, 4, 5, 6, 8)

and the

FOURTEENTH AMENDMENT
SECTIONS 1 AND 5

AMENDMENT I

Congress shall make no law respecting an establishment of religion, or prohibiting the free exercise thereof; or abridging the freedom of speech, or of the press; or the right of the people peaceably to assemble, and to petition the Government for a redress of grievances.

. . . . .

AMENDMENT IV

The right of the people to be secure in their persons, houses, papers, and effects, against unreasonable searches and seizures, shall not be violated, and no Warrants shall issue, but upon probable cause, supported by Oath or affirmation, and particularly describing the place to be searched, and the persons or things to be seized.

AMENDMENT V

No person shall be held to answer for a capital, or otherwise infamous crime, unless on a presentment or indictment of a Grand Jury, except in cases arising in the land or naval forces, or in the Militia, when in actual service in time of War or public danger; nor shall any person be subject for the same offence to be twice put in jeopardy of life or limb; nor shall be compelled in any criminal case to be a witness against himself, nor be deprived of life, liberty, or property, without due process of law; nor shall private property be taken for public use, without just compensation.

AMENDMENT VI

In all criminal prosecutions, the accused shall enjoy the right to a speedy and public trial, by an impartial jury of the State and district wherein the crime shall have been committed, which district shall have been previously ascertained by law, and to be informed of the nature and cause of the accusation; to be confronted with the witnesses against him; to have compulsory process for obtaining witnesses in his favor, and to have the Assistance of Counsel for his defence.

. . . . .

AMENDMENT VIII

Excessive bail shall not be required, nor excessive fines imposed, nor cruel and unusual punishments inflicted.

. . . . .

AMENDMENT XIV

Section 1. All persons born or naturalized in the United States, and subject to the jurisdiction thereof, are citizens of the United States and of the State wherein they reside. No State shall make or enforce any law which shall abridge the privileges or immunities of the citizens of the United States; nor shall any State deprive any person of life, liberty, or property, without due process of law; nor deny to any person within its jurisdiction the equal protection of the laws.

. . . . .

Section 5. The Congress shall have power to enforce, by appropriate legislation, the provisions of this article.

. . . . .

SELECTED PERTINENT STATUTES

from the

UNITED STATES CODE

18 USC §242 Deprivation of rights under color of law

Whoever, under color of any law, statute, ordinance, regulation, or custom, willfully subjects any inhabitant of any State, Territory or District to the deprivation of any rights, privileges, or immunities secured or protected by the Constitution or laws of the United States, or to different punishments, pains, or penalties, on account of such inhabitant being an alien, or by reason of his color, or race, than are prescribed for the punishment of citizens, shall be fined not more than $1,000 or imprisoned not more than one year, or both; and if death results shall be subject to imprisonment for any term of years or for life.

42 USC §1983 Civil action for deprivation of rights

Every person who, under color of any statute, ordinance, regulation, custom, or usage, of any State or Territory, subjects, or causes to be subjected, any citizen of the United States or other person within the jurisdiction thereof to the deprivation of any rights, privileges, or immunities secured by the Constitution and laws, shall be liable to the party injured in an action at law, suit in equity, or other proper proceeding for redress.

NOTES

NOTES